# Collected Classics

## Volume 4

Level 3

**Pearson Education Limited**
Edinburgh Gate, Harlow,
Essex CM20 2JE, England
and Associated Companies throughout the world.

ISBN 0 582 343615

This collection of classics first published 2000

*Sherlock Holmes and the Mystery of Boscombe Pool*
Text copyright © J.Y.K. Kerr 1991
Interior photographs copyright © David Cuzik 1991

*The Thirty-Nine Steps*
Copyright © Penguin Books 1999
Illustrations by Piotr Lesniak

*The Turn of the Screw*
Text copyright © Cherry Gilchrist 1996
Illustrations © Ian Andrew (Virgil Pomfret) 1996

*Jane Eyre*
Text copyright © Ann Ward 1991
Illustrations © Richard Johnson 1991

*Sense and Sensibility*
Text Copyright © Cherry Gilchrist 1997
Illustrations copyright © David Cuzik 1997

Typeset by Refine Catch, Suffolk
Set in 11/14pt Bembo
Printed in Spain by Mateu Cromo, S.A. Pinto (Madrid)

*All rights reserved; no part of this publication may be reproduced, stored
in a retrieval system, or transmitted in any form or by any means,
electronic, mechanical, photocopying, recording or otherwise, without the
prior written permission of the Publishers.*

Published by Pearson Education Limited in association with
Penguin Books Ltd, both companies being subsidiaries of Pearson Plc

## Contents

|  | page |
|---|---|
| Sherlock Holmes and the Mystery of Boscombe Pool | 1 |
| The Thirty-Nine Steps | 49 |
| The Turn of the Screw | 137 |
| Jane Eyre | 185 |
| Sense and Sensibility | 233 |

# Sherlock Holmes and the Mystery of Boscombe Pool

## SIR ARTHUR CONAN DOYLE

Level 3

Retold by J. Y. K. Kerr
Series Editors: Andy Hopkins and Jocelyn Potter

# Contents

|  | page |
|---|---|
| Introduction | 5 |
| Sherlock Holmes and the Mystery of Boscombe Pool | 9 |
| Activities | 46 |

## Introduction

*'Everything points to the fact that the young man is guilty, does it not?'
I said.*

*'The facts are not always what they seem,' answered Holmes. 'If we look at them in another way, they can tell quite a different story.'*

As usual, Sherlock Holmes has asked his friend Dr Watson to come with him to study another crime. As usual, it is Dr Watson who tells the story. A rich man, Charles McCarthy, is dead. He died near Boscombe Pool, hit on the head with something heavy. Who killed him? The police are sure that they know. Young Patience Moran saw Mr McCarthy and James, his son, by the lake. They were both shouting. James was very angry. He was lifting up his arm . . .

The facts are clear. But Sherlock Holmes is not so sure. The police have taken James away and he is in prison, waiting for the case to come to court. Holmes has to work fast to find the real murderer.

Arthur Conan Doyle was born in Edinburgh, Scotland, in 1859, one of seven children. He was a clever boy, who loved reading. After school he studied medicine at Edinburgh University. One of the teachers there was a doctor called Joseph Bell. Bell could look at a person and tell you what his job was. He had a scientific way of studying people's faces, movements and clothes. When Conan Doyle was writing about his great detective, he remembered Joseph Bell. Like Sherlock Holmes, Bell was tall and thin.

After he finished his studies, Conan Doyle first worked as a ship's doctor. Then he went to work in the south-west of England, near Portsmouth. He lived there for eight years. For part of this time, his younger brother, Innes, lived with him. Some people say that Conan Doyle used Innes for Dr Watson in his stories. Conan Doyle did not have much medical work, so he spent a lot of his time writing. His first book about Sherlock Holmes was *A Study in Scarlet*, which he wrote in 1887. He sent it to two companies but they sent the book back. A third company accepted it but paid Conan Doyle only £25! *The Sign of Four* came out three years later. But Conan Doyle's real success with Sherlock Holmes began in 1891 when he started to write short stories for the *Strand Magazine*. Later, these stories came out as complete books: first, *The Adventures of Sherlock Holmes* (1892) and then *The Memoirs of Sherlock Holmes* (1894).

Conan Doyle began to get tired of his detective and wanted to 'kill' him. In one story, Holmes had a fight with his greatest enemy, Professor Moriarty, and fell to his death in the Swiss mountains. Conan Doyle was unhappy that readers didn't show the same interest in his historical books like *The White Company* (1891) or his scientific adventure stories like *The Lost World* (1912). Everybody still preferred Holmes and Watson. Conan Doyle found that he had to bring Holmes back to life and write five more books about him. Each of these was an immediate success. In his later life, Conan Doyle became interested in sending and receiving messages to and from the world of the dead. He died in 1930, at the age of 71.

Conan Doyle was not the first person to write detective stories. He got the idea from one of his favourite writers, the American, Edgar Allan Poe. But Poe's French detective, Dupin, is almost unknown because Poe wrote only one short story about him, 'The Murders in the Rue Morgue'. Sherlock Holmes, on the other hand, is in over a hundred stories. Today, Holmes is still the world's most famous detective and one of the most famous people in English literature. The stories are on sale in many languages. There have been many plays, films, and television programmes about him. Everyone recognizes his long, unsmiling face, his special hat and special kind of pipe. 'He is all mind and no heart,' Conan Doyle once said. But for many readers Sherlock Holmes is like a real person. Since Conan Doyle died, people have written Sherlock Holmes's life story and made museums about him and his work. People from all over the world go to see his flat at 221B Baker Street, in central London.

*'Will you go?'* said my wife, looking across at me.

# Sherlock Holmes and the Mystery of Boscombe Pool

One morning, I was having breakfast with my wife when a telegram arrived. It was from Sherlock Holmes. It read:

*Are you free for a day or two? Must go to the west of England to help with the Boscombe Pool murder. Shall be glad if you can come with me. The change will be good for us. Leaving Paddington station on the 11.15 train.*

'Will you go?' said my wife, looking across at me.

'I really don't know what to say,' I answered. 'I have a lot of sick people to visit.'

'Anstruther can do your work for you. You are looking tired and I think a change from your work will be good for you. You are always so interested in Mr Holmes's cases.'

'As always, you are right, my dear. But if I do go, I must get ready immediately, because the train leaves in half an hour.'

My early life as a soldier taught me to travel with very few things. In a few. minutes, I was on my way to Paddington station. There I found my old friend in his long grey coat and his favourite hat. He was walking up and down the platform.

'It is really very good of you to come, Watson,' he said. 'I need a friend like you at times like this. No one can help me as you can. Please keep two corner places and I shall buy the tickets.'

We were alone during the train journey. Holmes had a large number of newspapers with him and for much of the time he wrote and thought. Finally, he made the papers

'Have you heard anything about this case?' he asked.

into a very large ball and threw them away, keeping only one.

'Have you heard anything about this case?' he asked.

'No, nothing. I have not seen a newspaper for some days.'

'The London papers have not written much about it. I have read them all because I need to know all the facts. It seems to be one of those cases which looks very clear. That is why I think it will be difficult.'

'Isn't that strange?'

'Oh no. Cases which seem very easy like this one are often the hardest, I find. But just now, things look very serious for the son of the murdered man.'

'So you are sure that it is a murder?'

'Not yet. It seems to be. But I must believe nothing until I have studied all the facts. Now I shall explain in a few words what I have read.

'Boscombe Valley is near Ross in Herefordshire. A large part of the land there belongs to a Mr John Turner. He made a lot of money in Australia and returned to live in England some years ago. His neighbour, Mr Charles McCarthy, was also in Australia and lives at Hatherley, a farm which belongs to Turner. The two men first met in Australia and it is natural that they have chosen to live in the same neighbourhood. Turner is the richer man and it seems that McCarthy pays him for the use of his farm. They seem to be good friends and spend quite a lot of their time together. McCarthy has one son, who is eighteen years old, and Turner has a daughter who is about the same age. The wives of both men are dead. The two families lived quietly and did not mix much with other people. McCarthy had two servants but Turner in his big house has several more – about six. That is all I have been able to find out about these families.'

'What about the murder, then?' I asked.

'Don't hurry me, Watson. Just listen. I am coming to that.

'Last Monday, 3 June, Charles McCarthy went to the town of Ross with his servant. This was in the morning. While he was there, he told his servant to hurry because he had an important meeting with someone at three o'clock that afternoon. They drove back quickly to his house at Hatherley. Just before three o'clock, McCarthy left the farmhouse and walked down alone to Boscombe Pool. He never came back.

'It is a quarter of a mile from Hatherley Farm to Boscombe Pool and two different people saw him as he walked that way. One was an old woman but we do not know her name. The other was a manservant of Mr Turner, called William Crowder. Both people say that McCarthy was alone. The servant also says that, a few minutes after he saw McCarthy go past, he also saw his son, Mr James McCarthy, going the same way. He had a gun under his arm. The son could see his father and was following him. But Crowder, the servant, thought nothing of this until he heard of McCarthy's death later that evening.'

'You explain it all so clearly,' I said.

'I have told you to listen, dear doctor. When I have finished, you can say what you like. I shall continue.

'Another person saw the two McCarthys after William Crowder. The land around Boscombe Pool is full of trees with a little grass in the open parts beside the water. A girl of fourteen, Patience Moran, was picking flowers among the trees that afternoon. She saw Mr McCarthy and his son close to the lake. They both seemed to be very angry. She heard Mr McCarthy using strong language to his son. She saw the young man lift up his arm. He seemed ready to hit his father. She felt so frightened that she ran away. When she got home, she told her mother about the quarrel. "When I saw them, they seemed to be going to have a fight," she said. Just as she was speaking, young

*Patience Moran saw Mr McCarthy and his son close to the lake.
They both seemed to be very angry.*

Mr McCarthy came running up to their house. "I have just found my father by the pool," he shouted. "He is dead. We must get help." He looked very excited, without either his hat or his gun. His right hand was red with blood. Immediately, Patience's parents went with him to the pool, where they found his father's dead body lying on the grass. There were many wounds in his head, made by something thick and heavy like the wooden part of the young man's gun. They found this gun lying on the grass not far from the dead man. The police soon came and immediately held the young man for questioning, then locked him up. His case will come up in a few weeks' time.'

'Everything points to the fact that the young man is guilty, does it not?' I said.

'The facts are not always what they seem,' answered Holmes. 'We think that they all point to the same thing but, if we look at them in another way, they can tell quite a different story. It is true that the case against the young man is very serious and maybe he is in fact guilty. But there are several people who believe that he is innocent. One of these is Miss Turner, the daughter of McCarthy's neighbour. She has asked Detective Lestrade to take on the case and now Lestrade, since he cannot really say no, has asked me to help him. That is why we are hurrying along in a train instead of having a quiet breakfast at home.'

'I am afraid that the case is so clear that no one will thank you for showing what happened,' I said.

'We shall see,' my friend answered. 'We both know that Lestrade is not as clever as he thinks and I am sure that I shall notice some things which he has missed. But there is something more to tell you. When the police came to Hatherley Farm and took young McCarthy prisoner, he said, "I am deeply sorry but I am not surprised. I was expecting this."'

*James McCarthy came running up to the Moran family's house and said, 'I have just found my father by the pool. He is dead.'*

'Of course, that shows that he is guilty,' I said.

'In no way. In fact, he has repeated many times that he is innocent.'

'But that is hard to believe, don't you think?'

'Of course not. He cannot be so stupid that he does not realize the danger which he is in. So he cannot be surprised that he is a prisoner. Clearly he is sorry that his father is dead and that they had a quarrel. His feelings are quite natural, I think.'

'So what story does this young man have to tell?'

'You can read it here in this newspaper,' said Holmes. He gave it to me and pointed to the right page. This is what I read:

Mr James McCarthy, the son of the dead man, gave the following story: 'I was away from home for three days because I had business in Bristol. I came back only last Monday in the morning. My father was not at home when I arrived. A servant told me that he was in Ross on business. After some time, I heard the wheels of his carriage coming back. I looked out of the window and saw him walking quickly away from the house. I did not know where he was going. I then took my gun and went for a walk. I wanted to shoot some birds in the trees on the other side of Boscombe Pool. On my way, I passed William Crowder, as he has told you. But he is wrong when he says that I was following my father. I had no idea that he was in front of me. When I was about a hundred yards from the pool, I heard someone call "Cooee!" My father and I often used this call. I hurried towards the pool and found him standing there. He seemed very surprised to see me and also quite angry. He asked, "What are you doing here?" I explained, we began to talk and more angry words followed. I became angry too. I felt ready to hit him but instead I decided to leave. I know that my father gets angry very quickly, sometimes about things that are not important.

I then went back towards Hatherley Farm. After only one hundred and fifty yards, I heard a terrible scream, so I ran back to the pool again. I found my father on the ground. He was dying. There were terrible wounds on his head. I dropped my gun and held him in my arms but he died almost immediately. I stayed beside him for some minutes and then I made my way to the nearest house to ask for help. I saw no one near my father when I returned with Mr and Mrs Moran. I have no idea how he got those wounds. He was a cold man and not much liked in the neighbourhood; but I do not think that he had any enemies. That is all I know about this business.'

Questioner: Did your father say anything to you before he died?

McCarthy: His voice was very weak. He spoke a few words but I only understood something about a rat.

Questioner: What did that mean to you?

McCarthy: It meant nothing. I do not think he knew what he was saying.

Questioner: What were you talking about with your father that made him so angry?

McCarthy: I prefer not to answer.

Questioner: I must ask you to tell us.

McCarthy: It is not possible for me to tell you. Please understand that it has nothing to do with his murder.

Questioner: That is for us to decide. If you do not answer, you must realize that the case against you will be worse.

McCarthy: I do not want to speak about it.

Questioner: Is it true that the call of 'Cooee' was a call which you and your father used between you?

McCarthy: Yes, it is.

Questioner: Then why did he use it before he saw you – before he even knew of your return from Bristol?

McCarthy: I do not know.

Questioner: Did you see anything unusual when you ran back to find your father?

McCarthy: Nothing very clear.

Questioner: What do you mean?

McCarthy: I was so surprised and worried that I could think only of my father. But I remember that, as I ran towards him, I saw something on the ground to the left of me. It seemed to be a piece of grey cloth – a kind of coat, I think. When I got up, I looked for it again but it was gone.

Questioner: Do you mean that it disappeared before you went for help?

McCarthy: Yes, it was gone.

Questioner: You cannot say what it was?

McCarthy: No, I just had a feeling that there was something there.

Questioner: How far from the body?

McCarthy: About fifteen yards away.

Questioner: And how far was it from the trees?

McCarthy: About the same.

Questioner: So you think that someone took it while you were only fifteen yards away?

McCarthy: Yes, but I had my back towards it.

The questioning of McCarthy ended here.

Looking at the newspaper, I said, 'I see that the questioner has used hard words about young McCarthy. He gives importance to the fact that his father called to him before he saw him and also that he did not want to explain his quarrel with his father. He tells us to remember the strange words which the dying man spoke. All these things, he says, are very much against the son.

Holmes laughed softly and made himself comfortable in his corner. 'Both you and the questioner have pointed to just those things which help the young man's case most. Don't you see that you believe him to be at the same time much too clever and not clever enough? He is not very clever if he cannot explain the quarrel in some way that makes us feel sorry for him. And too clever with his strange story of the rat, and the cloth which disappeared. No, Watson, I shall study this case with the idea that what the young man says is true. We shall see where that path takes us. And now I shall not speak another word about the case until we get to Ross. We shall have lunch at Swindon and that will be in twenty minutes.' Then Holmes took a book from his pocket and sat silently, reading.

It was nearly four o'clock when we arrived at last at the pretty little town of Ross. A thin man with an ugly face was waiting for us on the platform. I knew immediately that this was Lestrade, of Scotland Yard. We drove with him to an hotel, where we took rooms.

'I have asked for a carriage,' said Lestrade, as we sat drinking a cup of tea. 'I know, Mr Holmes, that you will not rest until you have visited the place of the murder.'

'A carriage? That was kind of you,' Holmes answered, 'but because of the weather I shall not need one.'

Lestrade looked surprised. 'I do not quite understand,' he said.

'There is no wind and not a cloud in the sky. I have a packet of cigarettes to smoke and the chairs in this hotel are unusually comfortable. I do not think that I shall need the carriage tonight.'

Lestrade gave a laugh. 'I am sure that you have decided how this case will end from your study of the newspapers. It is all quite clear and it becomes clearer with every new fact. Still, one

*A young woman hurried into the room. 'I have driven here to tell you this: I know that James did not do it.'*

has to please a young woman and this one knows what she wants. She has heard of you and she decided to ask you to come. I told her again and again that there is nothing that you can do which I have not already done but . . . Look, here is her carriage at the door!'

As he was speaking, a young woman hurried into the room: She was one of the prettiest girls that I have ever seen in my life. Her eyes were shining, her lips open, ready to speak, and her face was pink with excitement.

She looked at each of us carefully, and then turned to my friend. 'Oh Mr Sherlock Holmes,' she said. She seemed to know immediately who he was. 'I am so glad that you have come. I have driven here to tell you this: I know that James did not do it. I know it and I want you to know it too. Please be quite sure of that fact before you start your work. I have known him since we were both little children and I know his weaknesses better than anyone. But he is too soft-hearted to hurt a fly. Anyone who really knows him must believe that he is innocent.'

'I hope that we can show that to be true, Miss Turner,' said Sherlock Holmes. 'Believe me, I shall do everything possible.'

'But you have read the facts. You have studied the problem. You must see something wrong in what people are thinking. Some way of escape. Do you not believe that he is innocent?'

'I think that probably he is.'

'There, now!' she said, throwing back her head and turning to Lestrade. 'Do you hear that? He gives me hope.'

Lestrade looked unhappy. He clearly thought that Holmes was mistaken. 'I am afraid that my friend here is only guessing,' he said.

'But he is right! I know that he is right. James and his father had many quarrels about me. Mr McCarthy wanted us to get married. I have always loved James and he loves me but we are like brother and sister. He is still young and knows very little about life and . . . and . . . I mean, naturally he did not wish to marry just yet. So there were quarrels. I am sure that this was one of them.'

'And your father?' asked Holmes. 'Did he also want you to marry James?'

'No, he was against it too. Only Mr McCarthy wanted it.' Holmes was watching her carefully and we saw that her face suddenly became a deeper pink.

'Thank you for this information,' Holmes said. 'Can I come and visit your father tomorrow?'

'I am afraid that the doctor will say no.'

'The doctor?'

'Yes, haven't you heard? My poor father has not been strong

for many years but with his sadness about this murder he has become very ill. He is in bed and Dr Willows says that his case is serious. Mr McCarthy was the only person left who knew Father in the old days in Australia – when he was in Victoria.'

'Ha! In Victoria? That is important.'

'Yes, at the mines.'

'Of course. I understand that those were the goldmines where Mr Turner made his money.'

'That is right.'

'Thank you, Miss Turner. You have been a very great help to me.'

'You will tell me tomorrow if you have any news? I expect that you will go to the prison to see James. Oh Mr Holmes, if you do go, please tell him this: I know he is innocent.'

'I will, Miss Turner.'

'I must go home now because my father needs me. He is unhappy if I leave him. Goodbye and God help you in your work.' She hurried from the room and we heard her carriage moving away down the street.

'I am surprised at you, Holmes,' said Lestrade, after keeping silent for a few minutes. 'Why do you give her hope when she is sure to lose it only too soon? I am not soft-hearted, as you know, but I think you are being unkind.'

'I believe that there is a way of saving James McCarthy,' said Holmes. 'Have you an order to see him in the prison?'

'Yes, but only for you and me.'

'Then I shall change my plans and go out. We have still got time to take a train to Hereford and see him tonight?'

'Plenty of time.'

'Then let us go. Watson, I am afraid that you will be bored but I shall only be away for an hour or two.'

I walked with them to the station and then came back alone

through the streets of the little town to our hotel. There I sat and tried to read a book. But the story was so stupid that my thoughts kept returning to the Boscombe Pool mystery. I could not follow the story. Finally, I threw the book across the room and began to think only about the happenings of the day. Perhaps this unlucky young man's words were really true? In that case, what terrible thing happened between the time that he left his father and the time that he ran back to the pool, hearing his dying screams? Something very frightening, I was sure. But what was it? Maybe the shape of the wounds had something to tell me, as a doctor. I rang the bell and asked for the weekly newspaper, which had a description of them. The wounds were in a group on the back part of McCarthy's head, on the left side. Clearly the murderer hit him from behind. This fact made James McCarthy's story easier to believe, perhaps. They were face to face during their quarrel, he said. Of course, it was also possible that James hit him when his father turned his back. Still, I decided to give Holmes this information. Then there was the strange talk of a rat when the old man lay dying. It is unusual for a dying man to use words with no meaning. Probably he was trying to explain how it all happened. But what did it mean? I thought hard, trying to find an answer to the mystery; but I could not. Then there was the grey cloth which young McCarthy saw. If this was true, then perhaps the murderer dropped it – his coat maybe – when he was running away. But the son was sitting beside his father, just a few yards away and saw no one. So every part of the case seemed to bring more problems. Lestrade's ideas did not surprise me but I believed strongly in my friend Sherlock Holmes. 'He will find new facts,' I thought to myself, 'and I need not lose hope if each new fact points to young McCarthy's innocence.'

♦

*There I sat and tried to read a book. But my thoughts kept returning to the Boscombe Pool mystery. Finally I threw the book across the room.*

It was late before Sherlock Holmes returned. He came back alone because Lestrade was staying at a different hotel. I told him about the head wounds, a fact which he seemed to find interesting.

'The weather seems to be staying fine,' he said. 'We don't want any rain to fall before we can look at the ground. But we must rest and be fresh for important work of this kind. I did not want to begin it after that long journey. I have seen young McCarthy.'

'And what did you learn from him?'

'Nothing.'

'Couldn't he tell you anything?'

'Nothing, as I have said. At first, I thought that he must know the name of the murderer. He wanted to save him or her – that was my idea. But now I am sure that he knows as little as we do. I must say that he is not a very intelligent young man, even if he is good-looking and also, I think, good-hearted.'

'I do not think much of his taste,' I said, 'if he really does not want to marry Miss Turner.'

'Ah, that is a long, sad story. This boy is deeply in love with her. But two years ago he did a very stupid thing. Miss Turner was still at school then and away from home. He did not know her very well. James became friendly with a woman in Bristol who worked in a bar. He married her secretly. Even now, no one knows that he is married. So think of his feelings when his father told him again and again to marry Miss Turner! He dearly wanted to marry her but he knew that it was impossible. His father, as we now know, was a cold, hard man and James could not tell him about his wife. He has spent the last three days in Bristol with this bar woman and his father of course knew nothing about it. Remember that fact. It is very important. But something good has happened at last, because his wife has now left him. She read in the newspaper about his serious trouble and wants to have nothing more to do with him. She has written to say that she has

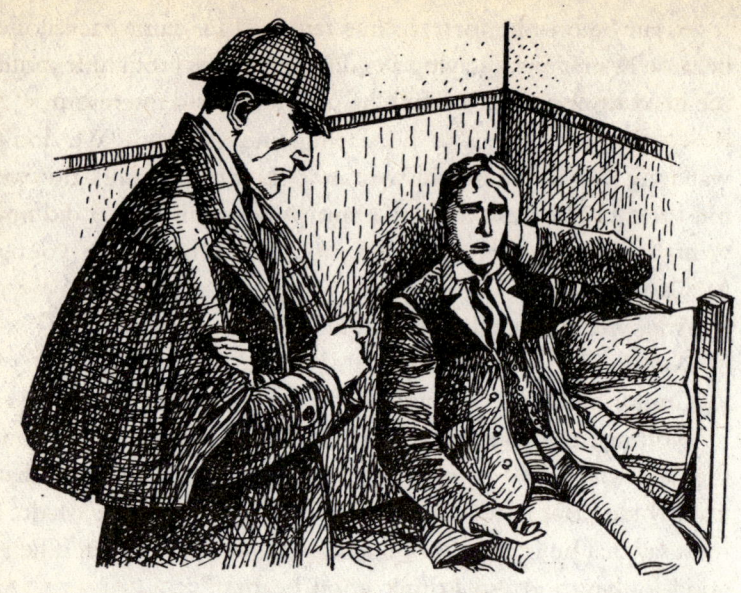

'I have seen young McCarthy. But now I am sure he knows as little as we do,' said Holmes.

a husband already – a sailor – and that she and James are not really married. This piece of news has made poor James a lot happier.'

'But if James is innocent, then who did the murder?'

'Ah, who? I want you to notice two important facts. The first is that the murdered man went to the pool to meet someone. This person was not his son, because his son was away from home. McCarthy did not know when his son was coming back. The second fact is that the murdered man called "Cooee!", not knowing about his son's return. Those are the two things which will help to save young James. And now let us change the subject. We shall talk no more of murders and leave all that business until tomorrow.'

Holmes was right: there was no rain during the night and the next day was bright and cloudless. At nine o'clock Lestrade came for us with the carriage and we left for Hatherley Farm and Boscombe Valley.

'There is serious news this morning,' said Lestrade; 'I hear that Mr Turner is dangerously ill. The doctor thinks that he is dying.'

'He is quite an old man, then?' asked Holmes.

'About sixty; but his health has been bad for some time. This business has made him really ill. He was an old friend of McCarthy's and helped him in a number of ways. I have learned that he gave him free use of Hatherley Farm.'

'Is that true? This is most interesting,' said Holmes.

'Oh yes, and he has helped him in other ways too. Everyone round here speaks of his kindness to McCarthy.'

'Really? Don't you think it strange then that McCarthy wanted his son to marry Turner's daughter? The Turners are rich and the McCarthys seem to be quite poor. We know that old Mr Turner has always been against the idea. His daughter told us that. Don't you find that McCarthy's friendliness is a little unusual?'

'You are always full of ideas, Mr Holmes,' said Lestrade, looking at me with a smile. 'I have come here to study the facts and they are difficult enough. Your thoughts always fly away from the real problems.'

'You are right,' said Holmes quietly. 'You do find it difficult to notice the facts.'

'Well, I have understood one fact which you do not seem to get hold of,' answered Lestrade, not very pleased.

'And that is?'

'That young McCarthy killed his father; any other way of seeing this case is just not possible.'

'Let us agree to disagree,' said Holmes, laughing. 'But if I am not mistaken, there is Hatherley Farm on the left.'

'Yes, that is it.'

It was a long, low building made of grey stone and it looked comfortable. But the windows were all shut and there was no smoke coming up from the roof. It looked empty. We knocked on the door and a young servant girl came out. She showed us first the boots which old Mr McCarthy was wearing at the time of his death. She also showed us a pair of the son's boots. Holmes studied their size and shape very carefully. He then asked to see the back of the house. From there we took the path which went to Boscombe Pool.

Holmes seemed to change as he hurried towards the place of the murder. He stopped being the quiet thinker of Baker Street. His face became redder and darker. His eyes shone with a hard light. He pressed his lips together and held his face down and his body low, studying the ground. His thoughts were turned so fully to the case that he did not seem to hear anything that we said. If he did, he answered only with a short word or two. He made his way quickly and silently along the path which went across the fields and then down through the trees to Boscombe Pool.

The ground was soft and wet as we got nearer. There were the marks of many feet both on the path and on the short grass on each side. Sometimes Holmes hurried on, sometimes he suddenly stood still. Once he walked away from the path into a field. Lestrade and I walked behind him. Lestrade seemed bored and uninterested in what Holmes was doing but I watched my friend carefully, knowing that every movement had a meaning.

Boscombe Pool is a small piece of water about one hundred and twenty yards wide. It lies at the end of the Hatherley Farm land where it joins the beautiful park land belonging to Mr Turner. Above the trees on the far side of the pool we could see the big red roofs of Turner's home. On the Hatherley

*Holmes studied the size and shape of the boots very carefully.*

*Holmes ran here and there like a dog which has smelled a wild animal.*

side of the pool the trees grew thick. There was a narrow piece of open ground about forty yards wide between the trees and the water of the lake. This open part was covered with short, wet grass. Lestrade showed us the place where the body was lying when they found it. In fact, the ground was so soft that I could see the marks left by McCarthy's fall. But, looking at Holmes, I realized from his excited face and the quick movement of his eyes that he was learning many other things from the marks on the grass. He ran here and there like a dog which has smelled a wild animal. Then he turned to the detective.

'Why did you go into the pool?' he asked Lestrade.

'I thought that maybe there was a gun or a piece of clothing or something like that in the water. But tell me, how. . .?'

'Oh come now, Lestrade. I have no time. That left foot of yours is everywhere. A child can see it. Look over there, where it disappears into the grass. This case was perfectly easy until a crowd of people came and stupidly walked all over the place. Here is where the Morans came and their footmarks have covered the ground for five or six yards around the body. But here are three different lines of the same feet.'

He took out a magnifying glass and lay down on top of his coat to see the marks better. Talking to himself more than to us, he said, 'These are young McCarthy's feet. Twice he was walking and once he was running fast, because his toes are pressing deeper into the ground. That follows his story, does it not? Then here are the father's footmarks as he walked up and down. What is this, then? Ha, ha! What have we here? Someone walking on his toes. In boots with square toes too. Quite unusual boots. They come, they go, they come again – of course, that was for the coat. Now, where did they come from?'

*He lay down and studied the ground with his magnifying glass.*

He ran up and down, sometimes losing and sometimes finding the line of footmarks. Soon we were standing in the shadow of a very big tree, the largest of them all. Holmes followed the marks to the far side of the tree. Then he lay down on his front again with an excited shout. For a long time, he stayed there, turning over the dry leaves until he picked up something small, which looked burned. He put this into an envelope. Next, he studied both the ground and the sides of the tree with his magnifying glass. A big rough stone was lying among the leaves. He looked at this too with great interest and kept it. Then he followed another line of footmarks. These went along a path through the trees until they came to a road; where the marks disappeared.

'It has been a most interesting case,' Holmes said, becoming himself again. 'I think that this little house on the right must be the Morans' home. I will go in and have a word with Mr Moran.

*A big rough stone was lying among the leaves. Holmes looked at this with interest and kept it.*

Perhaps I will write a short letter. After that we shall drive back to the town and have lunch. Please walk to the carriage. I shall be with you again in ten minutes.'

◆

Ten minutes later, we were in the carriage, driving back to Ross. Holmes was still carrying with him the stone, found among the trees. 'You will be interested in this,' he said to Lestrade, holding it out.

'I see no marks on it.'

'There are none.'

'How do you know that it is important, then?'

'The grass was growing under it. Clearly it was lying there for only a day or two. I could not find the place that it came from: there are too many stones around. But it is the right shape to make the wounds in McCarthy's head.'

'And the murderer?'

'He is a tall man, left-handed, with a bad right leg. He wears thick shooting boots and a grey coat, smokes Indian cigars, uses a cigar-holder and carries a pocket-knife – not a very sharp one. There is more information that I can give you; but that will be enough for you to find him, I think.'

Lestrade laughed. 'I am afraid I find all this hard to believe,' he said. 'This information is all very well but it does not show that a person is guilty of murder.'

'We shall see,' said Holmes. 'You work in your way and I shall work in mine. I shall be busy this afternoon and I shall probably go back to London on the evening train.'

'And leave the case unfinished?'

'No, finished.'

'But the mystery?'

'Is a mystery no more.'

'Who was the guilty person then?'

'Oh, God help us! The person I have just described, of course.'

'But who is he?'

'That will not be difficult to find out. The number of people who live in this neighbourhood is not large.'

Lestrade had a hopeless look on his face. 'I am a sensible man,' he said slowly. 'I really cannot run all over the place looking for a left-handed man with a bad leg. My friends at Scotland Yard will laugh at me.'

'All right,' said Holmes quietly. 'I have given you the information. Now here we are at your address, I believe. Goodbye. I shall send you a few words before I leave.'

We dropped Lestrade at his hotel and then drove to ours, where we found lunch upon the table.

'Look here, Watson,' said my friend when the meal was over. 'Just sit here in this chair and listen to me for a little. I am not sure what to do and your ideas will be useful. Light a cigar and I shall explain.'

'Please do.'

'Well, when we first learned about this case, there were two things that we both noticed immediately. They are both parts of young McCarthy's story. To me they showed him to be innocent. To you they seemed to make him guilty. The first thing is that his father called "Cooee" to him before he saw him. The second is that he spoke of a rat as he lay dying. He said several other words, you remember, but that was the only word that his son understood. Now these two facts must be the start of our thinking. We shall also begin by believing that the boy's story is perfectly true.'

'What about this "Cooee", then?'

'Well, clearly the father was not calling to his son. The son, as far as he knew, was in Bristol. It was just luck that James heard his father's call. The "Cooee" was for the person that old McCarthy was going to meet. But "Cooee" is a special call that Australians use. The person whom McCarthy expected to meet at Boscombe Pool was probably someone who knew Australia.'

'What about the rat, in that case?'

Sherlock Holmes took a piece of paper from his pocket and put it on the table. 'This is a map of Australia,' he said. 'I sent for it last night.' He put his hand over part of the map. 'What do you read?' he asked.

'A RAT,' I read.

'And now?' He lifted his hand.

'BALLARAT.'

'Quite right. That was the word which the old man spoke; but his son only understood the last part of it. He was trying to give the name of his murderer: Mr Something of Ballarat.'

'That's most surprising!' I said.

'It is perfectly easy,' said Holmes. 'And now, you see, the number of possible people immediately becomes much smaller. Someone who has a grey coat or jacket: that is another thing we can be sure about, if we believe the son's story. We have already come from knowing nothing to a picture of an Australian from Ballarat with a grey coat.'

'Quite true.'

'And this person felt at home in the valley, because it is only possible to get to the pool across other people's land. Strangers cannot usually go there.'

'Again you are right.'

'Then there is our visit today. By looking carefully at the ground I was able to describe the wanted man still more fully to that stupid detective Lestrade.'

'But how did you find out those other facts?'

'You know my ways. It is the very small things that I always look for.'

'You knew that he was tall, because the space between the

footmarks showed a man with long legs. And the marks also told you what kind of boots he wore.'

'Yes, they were unusual boots.'

'But his bad leg?'

'The mark of his right foot was always less clear than the mark of his left. He stood more heavily on the left because his right leg hurt him.'

'But you also say that he is left-handed?'

'Ah, yes! It was you, dear Watson, who noticed the kind of head wound which the doctor described. The murderer hit McCarthy from behind but on the left side of the head. This shows that he was left-handed. Try to do it with your right hand, if you do not believe me. During the quarrel between the father and son, he stood behind that big tree. He was smoking at the time. I found the ash from a cigar, which I know to be an Indian cigar, at the foot of the tree. You remember that smoking is one of my favourite subjects and that I have written a paper on the ash from one hundred and forty different kinds of pipes, cigars and cigarettes. I looked around and soon found the cigar end lying among the leaves. It was an Indian cigar, from a shop in Rotterdam.'

'And the cigar-holder?'

'I could see that he did not put the cigar end in his mouth, so I know that he uses a cigar-holder. The end was cut off, not bitten off, but the cut was not a clean one. This showed me that he used an old pocket-knife.'

'Holmes,' I said, 'you have described this man perfectly. Now he cannot escape and you have saved an innocent man's life. Now I see where all these facts are pointing. The guilty man is . . .'

◆

'Mr John Turner,' called out the hotel waiter, opening door of our sitting-room for a visitor.

The man who came in was strange and frightening to look at. He walked slowly and with difficulty. He looked sick; but his hard face, full of deep lines, and his heavy arms and legs showed that he was strong, both in body and in his feelings. His untidy beard, thick grey hair and dark eyes gave him a wild, proud look but his face was white as ash. I noticed the light blue colour of the skin around his nose and lips. As a doctor, I could see immediately that he was seriously ill.

'Please sit down on the sofa,' said Holmes softly. 'So you got my letter?'

'Yes, Moran brought it to me. It says that you want to see me here, because it will make things easier.'

'I think that people will talk if they see me going to your house.'

'And why do you want to see me?' He looked at my friend with sad, tired eyes. He seemed already to know the answer to his question.

'Yes,' said Holmes, answering his look more than his words. 'It is true. I know all about McCarthy.'

The old man hid his face in his hands. 'God help me!' he shouted. 'I did not want the young man to get hurt. If the case goes against him, I promise you that I shall tell the police everything.'

'I am glad to hear it,' said Holmes in a serious voice.

'I have not spoken yet only because of my dear girl. Maybe I — but no, it will break her heart if she hears that I am a prisoner.'

'Perhaps that need not happen,' said Holmes.

'What?'

'I am not a policeman. I understand that it was your daughter who asked me to come, so I am working for her. But,' and here he looked hard at Turner, 'you must save young McCarthy.'

*Holmes sat down at the table with a pen and some paper, 'Just tell us the true story,' he said.*

'I am a dying man,' said Turner. 'I have had diabetes for years. My doctor does not think that I have more than a month to live. But naturally I prefer to die under my own roof than in prison.'

Holmes stood up, crossed to the table and sat down at it with a pen in his hand and some paper in front of him. 'Just tell us the true story,' he said. 'I shall write it all down. You will put your name to it and Watson here will listen to everything. Then if I need to save young McCarthy's life, I can give it to the police. I promise you that I shall not use it until I must.'

'Very well,' said the old man. 'I do not think that I shall live until the case comes up, so it does not matter much to me. But I want to save Alice's feelings if I can. It is a terrible thing for her to live with. She is so young . . . And now I will explain everything to you. It has taken a long time to happen but it will not take me a long time to tell. You did not know this dead man, McCarthy. He was a true criminal – bad in every possible way. I hope that you never fall into the hands of someone like him. He has sat on my back for twenty years and he has made my life impossible. I shall tell you first how I met him and became tied to him and his greedy ways.

'It was in the early '60s at the mines. I was a young man then, hot-blooded and ready to try anything new. I made some bad friends, began drinking, had no luck in finding gold. So I left the mines and became what you call here a gangster – a robber on the roads. There were six of us and we had a wild, free life, robbing a sheep station sometimes or stopping the carriages on the road to the mines. Black Jack of Ballarat was the name I took and in Australia people still remember our group as the Ballarat Boys. One day, a carriage was carrying gold from Ballarat to Melbourne, so we hid beside the road and took it by surprise. There were six guards on horses and six of us, so we nearly lost the fight. But we shot four of them within a few minutes. They killed three of our boys before we got our hands on the gold. I put my gun to the head of the driver, who was this same man, McCarthy. I meant to shoot him but decided to let him go. I still remember his greedy little eyes looking hard at my face. He planned to remember me. We rode away with the gold and became rich men. I left my old friends and made my way back to England. Here no one knew me or my past. I decided to stop travelling and live a good and quiet life. A family wanted to sell that big house at Boscombe, so I bought it. I began to put my money to good uses, unlike the way I first got it. I also got married. My wife died young but she left me dear little Alice. Alice is all the world to me. Even when she was still a baby, her little hand seemed to show me the right way to live. She is the first person who has ever done that. In a word, I changed my selfish ways and did everything I

'One day, a carriage was carrying gold from Ballarat to Melbourne, so we hid beside the road and took it by surprise.'

could to become a better person. All was going well until McCarthy came along.

'I was in London on business one day and I met him by accident in Regent Street. He was almost without shoes on his feet or a coat on his back.

'"Here we are at last, Jack," he said, touching me on the arm. "We shall be like a family to you. There are two of us, me and my son, and you can look after us now. And if you do not – remember that this is England. There is always a policeman nearby to tell my story to."

'Well, they came down to the West Country and I could not shake them off. They lived without paying in the best farm that I had. There was no rest for me now, no forgetting. Everywhere I went, his greedy, smiling face was at my side. He asked for everything that he needed and I gave it to him without question: money, a house, a carriage. It got worse as Alice grew up. He soon realized that I was more afraid of her knowing my past than I was of the police. At last, he asked for the one thing I could not give. He asked for Alice. His son, you see, was a young man and Alice too was not a child any more. He thought it a wonderful idea for his son to have all my land and money, when he married Alice. But of course, I could not agree. I did not dislike the boy but his father's blood is in him and that is enough. I told McCarthy no – never. McCarthy was ready to go to the police. I told him to do his worst. We finally agreed to meet at the pool, half-way between our two houses. We were going to talk about McCarthy's plan one more time.

'When I went down there, I saw him talking to his son. They were having a quarrel about Alice. I hid behind a tree and smoked a cigar, because I needed to talk to Charles alone. But as I listened to his words, everything inside me that was black and angry seemed to break out. He was pressing his son to marry my daughter. It didn't seem to matter what my daughter's feelings were. He spoke of her as if she was a woman of the streets. It made me wild to think of my dearest child in the hands of that criminal. How could I break the tie? I was already a dying man with no hope left. My head was clear and my arms were still strong but I did not have long to live. But my daughter! And the picture she had of her loving father! I could save them both. I only had to stop that man's tongue from telling my secret. So I did it, Mr Holmes. I feel able to do it again, right or wrong. I have done many bad things in my life but I have paid for them. I could not stand still and see my innocent daughter so hurt. I hit him and he fell. To me he seemed nothing more than an animal. His screams brought his son running back but by this time I was among the trees. Of course, I had to go back and get my coat, which I dropped as I hurried away. That is the true story, Mr Holmes, the story of everything that happened. Now, show me that paper.'

'Well, it is not for me to speak of right or wrong,' said Holmes, as the old man wrote his name at the bottom of the last page. 'I hope that I shall never have to show that you are guilty.'

'I hope not, sir. And what do you mean to do now?'

'Because of your health, I shall do nothing. You know too well that you must live with your terrible past.' Holmes pointed to the handwritten pages on the table. 'I will keep this information and if they decide that young McCarthy is guilty of this murder, I must of course use it. If that does not happen, no man alive shall ever see it. Your secret will be safe with us. And the mystery of Boscombe Pool will stay a mystery for ever.'

'Goodbye, then,' said the old man in a broken voice. 'When your time comes, you will be able to die knowing that you have done a great kindness.'

His great sick body was shaking as he slowly left the room.

'It is not for me to speak of right or wrong,' said Holmes, as the old man wrote his name at the bottom of the last page.

'God help us,' said Holmes, after keeping silent for some time. 'Why is life so hard on poor old men like him? Every time that I meet a case like this, I say to myself: "There but for the goodness of God goes Sherlock Holmes."'

James McCarthy's case came up some weeks later. The decision was: not guilty of murder. The few facts which Holmes gave to the police were enough to free him. Old Turner lived for seven months more but he is now dead. It seems that James and Alice will soon become husband and wife, knowing nothing of that great black cloud that rests over the past.

# ACTIVITIES

**Pages 9–24**

*Before you read*
1 Look at the pictures in this part of the story.
   a When does the story happen?
      100 years ago? 50 years ago? 10 years ago?
   b Which pictures show Sherlock Holmes?
2 All these words come in the first part of the story. Choose the right meaning for each from the list a–i below.
   *alone   carriage   case   guilty   innocent*
   *mine   quarrel   servant   telegram   wound*
   a shown by law to be a criminal
   b a way of travelling before there were cars
   c somebody who works for other people in their home
   d shown by law not to be a criminal
   e a fight using words only
   f a hole or cut in the body
   g a place where men get metal out of the ground
   h a problem, e.g. a crime, that detectives have to study
   i a very quick kind of message, not used today

*After you read*
3 Can you name these people?
   a the murdered man
   b his neighbour, living near Boscombe Pool
   c a young man held by the police
   d a young woman, daughter of 'b' above
   e a girl who saw a family quarrel
   f a police detective
   Which two of these people are in love?
4 Why do the police think that James McCarthy is the murderer?

**Pages 25–37**

*Before you read*

5 Write sentences to show the meaning of these words from the story:
   a mark / path
   b ash / cigar / magnifying glass
6 Look at the picture on page 29.
   a What is the name of the building?
   b Why do you think that Holmes is looking at boots and shoes?

*After you read*

7 Copy this map of the Boscombe Valley. Then draw the movements of Sherlock Holmes on the day that he visited Boscombe Pool. Start from Hatherley Farm and finish where the carriage was waiting.

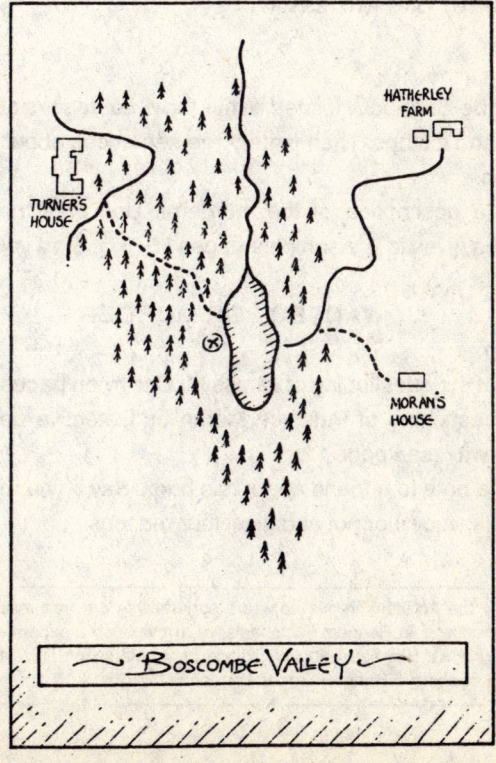

8 Holmes knows these things about the murderer:
   a he is left-handed
   b he smokes Indian cigars
   c he has a bad right leg
   Explain how Holmes finds out these facts.

## Pages 38–45

*Before you read*

9 Can you guess the name of the murderer? Why did he or she kill Mr McCarthy? Discuss your ideas with other students.

*After you read*

10 How does Australia come into the story? Use just one sentence for your answer.
11 Why does Holmes decide to keep the true story of the murder from the police? Give two reasons.

## Writing

12 Describe Sherlock Holmes. Write three sentences about his face, body and clothes. Then write three sentences about Holmes as a person.
13 Write a description of the murderer. Use only the facts which Holmes gives to Watson (see pages 35–37). Start your description like this:

   WANTED FOR MURDER

   A man . . .
14 Look at the questioning of James McCarthy on pages 17–18. Write the questioning of Patience Moran by Detective Lestrade in the same way (see page 12).
15 Write a note to a friend about this book. Say if you think that he or she will enjoy it or not and give your reasons.

---

Answers for the Activities in this book are published in our free resource packs for teachers, the Penguin Readers Factsheets, or available on a separate sheet. Please write to your local Pearson Education office or to: Marketing Department, Penguin Longman Publishing, 5 Bentinck Street, London W1M 5RN.

# *The Thirty-Nine Steps*

## JOHN BUCHAN

Level 3

Retold by Roland John
Series Editors: Andy Hopkins and Jocelyn Potter

# *Contents*

|  |  | page |
|---|---|---|
| Introduction | | 53 |
| Chapter 1 | The Man Who Died | 55 |
| Chapter 2 | The Milkman | 58 |
| Chapter 3 | The Innkeeper | 62 |
| Chapter 4 | The Adventure with Sir Harry | 70 |
| Chapter 5 | The Roadman Who Wore Glasses | 79 |
| Chapter 6 | The Man with the Strange Eyes | 86 |
| Chapter 7 | The Fisherman | 96 |
| Chapter 8 | The Black Stone | 105 |
| Chapter 9 | The Thirty-Nine Steps | 113 |
| Chapter 10 | The House by the Sea | 119 |
| Activities | | 131 |

## *Introduction*

John Buchan was born in Scotland in 1875. He was educated at the universities of Glasgow and Oxford. He then studied law, and after this he had many different jobs. He worked as a reporter and a businessman, and he also held important political and government posts. He spent parts of his life in South Africa, France and Canada. In his free time, he succeeded in writing a large number of books. He was given the title of Baron Tweedsmuir and died in 1940 in Montreal. At that time he was the Governor-General of Canada.

Buchan wrote short stories and longer books, historical fiction and stories of the present day. He produced factual books: *Nelson's History of the War* (1915–19), for example, was a very long work in 24 books. He also wrote about the life and work of famous people like Oliver Cromwell and the writer Sir Walter Scott. Later Buchan's readers were able to read about his own life in *Mercury Hold-the-Door*, which came out after his death.

Most people know Buchan's name for his stories of mystery and adventure. Five of his spy books are about the adventures of Richard Hannay. The first and most famous of these is *The Thirty-Nine Steps* (1915). In this year the world was watching the terrible war (the Great War or the First World War) in Europe. *The Thirty-Nine Steps* was written during this time. It is a great spy story with lots of action. Much of this action takes place in the green empty spaces of the Scottish Highlands. Alfred Hitchcock chose the book for the film of the same name. The film was made in 1935. It was, and is today, very popular.

In the story, Richard Hannay has just returned to London from Rhodesia, in East Africa. One day he is visited by a mysterious man who asks for his help. When he agrees, it is the start of Hannay's adventures. These take him hundreds of kilometres across England and Scotland. His life is in danger from a group of foreign spies and his country is in danger from their secret plans. He finds himself running from both the spies and the police. His only hope is to reach some of the highest people in the land. But will they believe his story?

## Chapter 1  The Man Who Died

My name is Richard Hannay and I am thirty-seven years old.

I was born in Scotland, but in 1883 my family moved to Rhodesia. I grew up in Africa and worked hard for 20 years. Then, in March 1914, I returned to Britain. That was five months before the First World War began. I brought a lot of money with me and I wanted to have a good time. Britain was the centre of all my dreams and plans, and I hoped to stay there for the rest of my life.

In May I was living in a flat in London. One evening I was alone there, reading the newspaper. I was interested in a story about Karolides, the Greek Prime Minister.

'He's a good man,' I thought to myself, 'and he's honest too. He's probably the strongest Prime Minister in Europe, and the Germans hate him.'

The sound of the door bell interrupted my reading. I put down the newspaper and opened the door. A man was standing outside. He was a thin man with a brown beard and small blue eyes. I did not know his name, but he had a flat on the top floor of the building.

'Can I speak to you?' he asked. 'May I come in for a minute?'

I invited him in and shut the door. He seemed very nervous.

'I'm very sorry,' he said. 'But I'm in trouble. Will you help me?'

'Well, I'll listen to you,' I said. 'But I can't promise more than that.'

I mixed a strong drink for him and he drank it quickly. When he put down the glass, he broke it.

'Sorry,' he said. 'I'm rather nervous tonight and there's a good reason for that. Now you seem honest, sir. You look like a man who is not easily frightened. Well, I'm in great trouble and I need a good friend.'

'Tell me about it,' I said, 'and then I'll give you my answer.'

'I'm an American,' he said. 'A few years ago I came to Europe to work for an American newspaper. I learned several languages and discovered quite a lot about European politics. I also found out about the German plans for war and I know a group of German spies. Well, these spies are looking for me now, and that's my problem. If you know anything about politics, sir, you'll know this. Europe is very near to war, and there's only one man who can stop it.'

'Who is he?' I asked.

'Karolides, the Greek Prime Minister.'

'Oh, I've just read something about him,' I said. 'There's a story in the evening paper.'

'Yes. Well, the Germans want to kill him,' he said. 'They will kill me too if they can. Karolides is going to come to London next month and he is going to visit the Foreign Office on 15 June. They've chosen that date to kill him. I'm the only man who can save him.'

'And how can I help you, Mr–?'

'Scudder,' he said. 'Franklin P. Scudder. I've just told you, sir, that these spies want to kill me. I thought that I was quite safe from my enemies in London. But yesterday evening I found a card in my letterbox, and there was a man's name on it. It was the name of one of the spies, my worst enemy.'

'You should tell the Foreign Office,' I said. 'They'll help you and perhaps they can save Karolides too.'

'There's no time for that. My enemies know that I'm in this building. They're probably waiting outside. Do you think that I can hide in your flat, sir?'

'Well, I want to check your story first,' I said. 'I'll go outside and look around. If I see anything unusual, I'll agree to help you. Is that all right?'

I left the flat and went out into the street. A man was standing outside the building. He lifted his hand when he saw me. I looked around quickly and saw a face at a window across the street. The man's sign was answered, and the face moved away from the window. I bought another newspaper at the corner of the street and then went back to the flat.

'All right, Mr Scudder,' I said. 'You can stay here tonight. I've checked your story. There's a man outside who is acting rather strangely. I think that your enemies are staying in the house across the street.'

Scudder stayed quietly in my flat for several days. When I went out, he was very nervous. There was always someone standing outside the building. I saw the face at the window opposite mine a few times, but nobody came to the flat. Scudder read and smoked. He filled a little black book with notes, and counted the days to 15 June.

One day he said, 'Time is passing quickly, Hannay. While they're watching the house, I won't be able to get away. If they catch me, will you continue the fight?'

I liked Scudder's adventures, and his story was exciting. But I had no interest in politics. He continued to talk, and I listened to some of it. He told me about a woman by the name of Julia Czechenyi, who was one of the spies. 'She's a terrible enemy, Hannay,' he said, 'but the old man is worse.'

This old man was Scudder's chief enemy, and he described him very clearly. 'It's strange,' he said, 'but he has the voice of a young man. And his eyes, Hannay! When you see his eyes, you never forget them. They're small and often half shut, like the eyes of a bird.'

He talked for a long time that day. I cannot remember everything that he said. But I knew that he was more nervous than usual.

In the evening I went out to dinner with a friend. It was half past ten when I returned. I opened the door of the flat and went in. The lights were not lit and this seemed rather strange. I put them on and looked around. There was nobody there, so I thought that Scudder was already in bed.

I walked into the next room and saw something in the corner. For a moment I could not see what it was. Then I suddenly felt very cold and weak. I wanted to open my mouth and cry out. But I could not move or say anything. Scudder was lying on his back with a knife through his heart.

## Chapter 2  The Milkman

I sat down and felt very sick. I sat there for perhaps five minutes and then fear brought me to my feet again. Scudder's white face was too much for me. I covered the body with a tablecloth. I found a drink and sat down again to think. Scudder was dead and his body proved his story. His enemies killed him because he knew their plans.

'They'll kill me next,' I thought. 'They know that he lived on the top floor. They know that he was staying in my flat. And they'll guess that he told me their plans.'

What could I do? Well, I could go to the police and tell them the story. But there was the problem of Scudder's death. 'The police will think that I killed him,' I thought.

I thought about it for a long time and then I formed a plan. I did not know Scudder very well, but I liked him. I enjoyed an adventure too, and I wanted to continue his work.

'I could write to the Prime Minister,' I thought, 'or to the Foreign Office. But perhaps that won't be necessary. I'll go away for a few weeks. Then I'll come back to London and go to the police.'

I went over to Scudder's body and took off the cloth. I

*Scudder was lying on his back with a knife through his heart.*

searched his pockets for his book of notes, but the book was not there. He had no other papers.

I opened my desk and took out a map of Britain. I thought that Scotland was the best place for my plan. I was born there and I spoke like a Scotsman. I spoke German very well too, and I thought about going to Germany. But perhaps Scotland was a better idea.

I chose Galloway, which was an empty part of the country. There were few big towns there, and it was not too far. I knew that there was a train to Scotland in the morning. It left London at ten minutes past seven. But how could I get out of the flat? Scudder's enemies were probably outside the building, so I had to leave secretly.

Then suddenly I had a great idea. Every morning at half past six the milkman brought my milk. He was a young man and we were the same size. He wore a white hat and coat. My idea was to borrow his clothes and the can of milk. Then I could get away from the building dressed as the milkman.

I went to bed and slept for a few hours. In the morning I counted my money and put fifty pounds in my pocket. While I was getting ready, I remembered my tobacco. I put my fingers into the large tobacco box and felt something hard under the tobacco. It was Scudder's little black book, and I put it in my pocket. It was a good sign, I thought. Scudder hid it there, and his enemies did not find it.

It was twenty minutes to seven now, and the milkman was late. But suddenly I heard the noise of the milk can on the stairs, and I opened the door.

'Come in, please,' I said. 'I want to speak to you.'

He came into the flat, and I shut the door.

'Listen,' I said, 'you're a good man, and I want you to help me.' I took a pound out of my pocket and added, 'If you agree, I'll give you this.'

When he saw the pound, his eyes opened wide.

'What do you want me to do?' he asked.

'I want to borrow your clothes and your milk can for a few minutes,' I said.

He laughed. 'What do you want them for?' he asked.

'I can't explain now. Let me borrow the things, and I'll be back in ten minutes.' I put the pound into his hand.

'All right,' he said. 'I like a bit of fun too.'

I put on his clothes and we went out of the flat. I shut the door behind me.

'Don't follow me,' I said. 'I'll soon be back.'

I went down the stairs and into the street. I made a noise with the milk can and began to sing. A man who was standing outside looked at me. He did not say anything. I looked at the house across the street and saw the face at the window again. I turned into another street and began to run. Then I took off the milkman's clothes and threw them, and the milk can, over a wall.

When I arrived at the railway station, it was ten minutes past seven. The train was moving slowly out of the station, and I had no time to buy a ticket. I ran towards it and caught the handle of a door. I opened it with difficulty and climbed into the train.

The ticket-collector soon came along. He was angry with me, and I had to give him some excuse. But he accepted it and wrote a ticket to Newton-Stewart in Galloway.

## Chapter 3  The Innkeeper

All that day I travelled. The train stopped at Leeds station, where I bought some food and the morning newspapers. Another ticket-collector told me that I had to change trains at Dumfries.

I read the papers, but of course there was nothing in them about Scudder's death. It was too early for that. Then I took out Scudder's little book. It was full of numbers, but there were also a few strange names. The words "Hofgaard", "Luneville", "Avocado" and "Pavia" were written there. "Pavia" was there several times.

It was clearly some kind of code, and I am very interested in codes. I thought about this one. I could see that there were numbers in place of letters. But what did the names mean? I knew that some of them were towns. But what code was used for people's names? There is usually a key word in codes like this, and I tried to guess it. "Hofgaard" was clearly not the key word, because it did not fit the rest of the code. I tried the other words too but none of them fitted.

I slept for an hour or two, and then the ticket-collector's voice woke me up.

'Be quick, sir. You have to change here.'

I looked out of the window. We were at Dumfries station. I got out and walked across to the Galloway train.

The train was quite full, and I had an interesting conversation with a farmer. He thought that I was a farmer too! We talked about animals and the price of milk and flour. People got out at different stations, but I continued. At five o'clock the train stopped at a small place and I liked the look of it. I cannot remember its name, but it was quiet. And it was a long way from London.

I left the train and the railway man's child took my ticket. It was a fine evening and I felt quite happy. I followed the road for about a kilometre and then took a path by a river. It was not long before I reached a small house. There was a woman at the door of the house and I spoke to her.

'May I stay here tonight?' I asked.

'You're welcome,' she replied. 'Please come in.'

Very soon she placed a fine meal in front of me, and I drank several glasses of thick, sweet milk.

When it grew dark, her husband came home. He was a big man with thick black hair. We talked for an hour or more, and smoked some of my tobacco. They did not ask me any questions. Perhaps they also thought that I was a farmer.

In the morning I enjoyed a large breakfast. But when I offered a pound to the woman, she refused to take it. It was a warm day, so she gave me a small can of milk to take with me. It was nine o'clock when I left the house.

I walked a few kilometres to the south because I wanted to return to the railway. But of course I could not go back to the same little station. The railway men and the child knew my face. I did not want them to remember me. So I went towards the next station and on my way there I formed a plan. The safest way was to return to Dumfries. If the police were searching for me, I was safer in a big town.

When I reached the station, I bought a ticket to Dumfries. I did not have long to wait until a train came in. I got in with an old man and his dog, and the man soon went to sleep. I borrowed his morning paper, which lay on the seat next to him. The story of the murder was on the first page in big letters: MURDER IN A LONDON FLAT.

The milkman, the paper said, waited for me for half an hour. Then he called the police. They arrived at my flat and found Scudder's body. The milkman was arrested and taken to prison. I felt very sorry for the poor man.

The story continued on the back page. And the latest news

was that the milkman was out of prison. The police were now looking for a man named Richard Hannay! They believed that he was on his way by train to Scotland. I was happy that the milkman was free. He knew nothing about the murder, and he only got a pound for his trouble.

The train stopped at a station which I already knew. It was the place where I got out the night before. Three men were talking to the railway men and the child. I watched them. The child was showing them the road that I took.

The train started again. While it was moving out of the station, I covered my face with the newspaper. It travelled about a kilometre and it suddenly stopped again. We were not at a station. The train was near a bridge over a river. This was my chance, and I changed my plan. I opened the door and jumped out. But the old man's dog tried to follow me. The old man woke up and ran to the door.

'Help! Help!' he cried.

I ran down to the river bank and hid in some long grass there. The ticket-collector and a number of other people were standing at the open door.

A lucky chance saved me. I could now see that the dog was tied to the man. Suddenly the dog jumped out of the train and pulled the old man out too. They fell down the bank, and everybody forgot me for a moment. They picked up the old man, and in the excitement the dog bit somebody. I took my chance and ran away through the long grass.

When I looked back, the excitement was over. People were climbing into the train again, and soon it began to move.

I walked along the river bank and thought about my problem. I was safe but I was also frightened. I do not mean that I was afraid of the police. I was thinking about Scudder's enemies and their plans. I felt sure that they wanted to kill me. Perhaps they wanted to see me in prison. They were a real danger to me, and I felt very frightened. My troubles were not over yet.

*The old man's dog tried to follow me.*

I climbed up from the river and I reached the top of a hill. There were other hills around me, and I could see clearly for several miles. There was the railway station and one or two houses. A road ran from the station towards the east. Then I looked up into the blue sky, and my heart almost stopped beating. A small plane was flying towards me. And I knew that Scudder's enemies were in that plane. The British police never used planes to look for people.

I hid behind a rock and watched. The plane flew up and down the river bank. It was so low that I could see a man inside. But I was sure that he did not see me. Then it climbed and turned. It flew over the river again and went back to the south. I decided to leave those hills. There was no place for me to hide. And I had no chance against a plane.

At six o'clock I reached the road. I followed it for a few kilometres. It was beginning to get dark when I came to a house standing alone next to a bridge.

A young man was on the bridge reading.

'Good evening,' he said. 'It's a fine evening, isn't it?'

'Yes, it is,' I replied. 'Is this house an inn?'

'Yes, sir, and I'm the innkeeper. Would you like to stay here tonight?'

'You're a very young innkeeper, aren't you?'

'Well, my father died last year and left me this inn. I'm living here with my mother but I don't like the work at all. I prefer to write stories, but what can I write about? I don't meet many interesting people.'

I suddenly had the idea that this young man could help me. 'I'll tell you a story,' I said, 'and it's true too. I need a friend. And I'll tell you this story if you help me. I'll give you permission to write it down, but don't do anything before 15 June. That's a very important date.'

Then I sat on the bridge and told him a story. He listened, and his eyes shone with excitement.

'I'm a farmer from Rhodesia,' I said, 'and I came to Britain a few weeks ago. I travelled by ship from German West Africa. The Germans there thought that I was a spy. They followed me all the way to Britain. They've already killed my best friend, and now they're trying to kill me. Have you read the newspaper today?'

'Yes.'

'Well then, you know about the murder of Franklin Scudder.'

The young man's eyes opened wide.

'He was my best friend, and he was killed in my own flat.'

I told him that Scudder was working for the Foreign Office before his death. And I explained that he told me some of the Germans' secrets. It was quite a long story, and I made it very exciting. At the end I said, 'You're looking for adventure, aren't you? Well, you've found it now. These German spies may come here, and I want to hide from them.'

He took my arm and pulled me towards the inn. 'You'll be safe here, sir,' he said. 'Tell me your adventures again, and I'll write them down.'

'All right. But I have some work to do first. Scudder gave me a long message in code. And I have to find out what it means.'

While we were going into the inn, I heard the plane again. It was flying low towards the bridge.

I had a quiet room at the back of the house. The innkeeper's mother brought me my meals. This place suited me very well.

The next morning I took out Scudder's notebook and began to work. The code was a difficult one, and I had to try many possible key words. By midday I knew where the spaces between the words were. I did not yet know the letters.

After dinner I tried again and worked hard until three o'clock. Then suddenly I had an idea. I was lying back in my chair when a woman's name came into my head. It was Julia Czechenyi, one of Scudder's worst enemies. Perhaps her name was the key word. I tried it quickly on the code and it was right!

"Julia" has five letters, and these letters were used in place of *a, e, i, o* and *u*. *J* is the tenth letter in English, and so he used the number ten to mean *a*. The letter *e* was the *u* of "Julia", and *u* is the twenty-first letter. So Scudder wrote the number 21 for *e*.

The name "Czechenyi" gave me nine other numbers, and I could soon read Scudder's notes. I sat in my room working quietly all afternoon. The facts in Scudder's little book were terrible. By the time the woman brought my tea, I was a very nervous man. My face looked pale, and I did not want to eat anything.

'Are you all right, sir?' she asked. 'You look ill.'

'Oh, it's nothing,' I said. 'Please put the things on the table.'

There was a sudden noise outside the inn, and the woman left my room. I heard a car stopping and then there were voices downstairs. A few minutes later the innkeeper ran into my room. 'Two men have just arrived,' he said, 'and they're looking for you. They described you very well.'

'What did you tell them?'

'I told them that you stayed here last night but left early this morning.'

'Can you describe them?'

'One is a thin man with dark eyes, and the other is rather fat.'

'Do they talk like Englishmen?'

'Oh, yes, I think so.'

I picked up a bit of paper and wrote quickly in German:

*Black Stone. Scudder knew about this, but he could not act until 15 June. Karolides is unsure of his plans, and I probably cannot help. But I will try if Mr T thinks I should*

Then I tore the sides of the paper. It looked like part of a private letter.

'Give this to them,' I said. 'Tell them that you found it in my room.'

Three minutes later the men drove away in the car. The innkeeper came back in great excitement.

'Your paper gave them a surprise,' he said. 'The dark one turned pale, and the fat one looked very ugly. They paid for their drinks and left.'

'Now I want you to do something for me,' I said. 'Get on your bicycle and go to the police at Newton-Stewart. Describe the two men and talk about the London murder. You can make something up. You can say that you heard a conversation between them. One man told the other that he was just out of prison. And say that you also heard Scudder's name. It isn't finished yet. Those two men will come back tomorrow morning, and the police have to be here to arrest them.'

He ran for his bicycle, and I continued my work on Scudder's notes. It was six o'clock when he returned.

'It's all right,' he said. 'The police will be here at eight o'clock in the morning.'

We had a meal together, and I had to tell him my adventures again. He made notes about them during the meal. I could not sleep that night. I finished Scudder's book and then sat up in my chair until morning. I was thinking about Scudder's terrible story.

At eight o'clock three policemen arrived at the inn. The innkeeper met them and showed them the garage. They left their car there and then came into the inn.

Twenty minutes later another car stopped a little way from the inn. I was watching from a window above the front door. The car was driven under some trees and left there. Two men got out of it and walked towards the inn.

My plan was not a very good one. I wanted the police to arrest the men. Then I was safe. But now I had a better idea. I wrote a note to the innkeeper and left it in my room. Then I opened my window and dropped quietly into the garden. I ran across the grass and along the side of a field. A few minutes later I reached the trees.

The car was standing there, and I got in. I started it and drove away. The wind carried the sound of angry voices to my ears. But soon I was travelling along that road at 80 kilometres an hour.

## Chapter 4   The Adventure with Sir Harry

It was a beautiful morning, but I was not thinking about the fine weather or the views around me. My thoughts were all of Scudder and his notes.

I knew now that Scudder lied to me in my flat. He told me a lot about Karolides, and part of it was true. But he did not tell me his really important secrets. Perhaps he was afraid to tell anyone. Of course Karolides was in danger, but the danger to Europe itself was greater! That was the real secret which Scudder kept in his little book.

The words "thirty-nine steps" were there several times in his notes. In one place he wrote: "Thirty-nine steps. I counted them. High tide 10.17 p.m." What did it mean? The "thirty-nine steps" were somewhere on the coast; the word "tide" proved that. But why were these steps important?

Scudder's notes said that there was definitely going to be a war. Nobody could stop it. The Germans had their plans ready years before, in February 1912. They planned to kill Karolides and to use his death as the excuse for war. "The Germans will talk about calm in Europe," he wrote, "but they're ready for war. They're going to attack us suddenly."

Scudder also wrote about the visit of a French officer to London. He was the head of the French army and was coming

*I opened my window and dropped quietly into the garden.*

on 15 June. "This officer will learn about the British plans and will then return to France." Scudder added that the Black Stone, the group of German spies, were also going to be in London on that same day. They hoped to learn about the plans too and to send them to Germany. When he died, Scudder was trying to stop them.

I drove on through the pretty villages of Galloway. It was a beautiful part of Scotland. But I could not enjoy the calm that was all around me. I had to get away from my enemies and stop them killing me. I had to find a way to continue Scudder's work. But it was going to be very difficult. The police and the "Black Stone" were after me, and I had no friends in Scotland.

At midday I came to a large village. I was very hungry and I decided to stop there. Then I saw a policeman. He was standing outside the Post Office, reading a telegram.

When he saw my car, he lifted his hand. At the same time he ran into the middle of the road.

'Stop! Stop!' he shouted.

I suddenly knew that the telegram was about me. After their conversation at the inn, perhaps the police accepted the spies' story. The spies probably described me and the car, and the police then sent telegrams to officers in all the villages.

I did not stop. The policeman put out his hand and ran along at the side of the car. He caught my arm through the window, which was open. I hit him very hard and he fell back into the road. I drove into the country again.

I drove up and down several hills. I was tired and hungry. I began to look for a quiet inn where I could rest. But suddenly there was a noise above me and I looked up. The plane was a few kilometres away, flying towards me. I drove fast down a hill between the trees. A car drove out from a side road, and I could not stop. I pulled the wheel hard to the right and shut my eyes.

My car ran through the trees and started to fall. I saw a river

15 metres below me. I jumped out of the car and fell into the grass. There was a terrible noise as the car turned over several times. Then it lay like a pile of old metal on the river bank.

Someone took my hand and pulled me out of the grass. A kind voice said, 'Are you hurt?'

A tall young man was standing there. 'I'm very sorry about this,' he said. 'I saw your car, but neither of us could stop in time. I hope that you're all right. But you look quite pale.'

I was rather pleased about the accident. The police were looking for that car, so I could not travel far in it now.

'I was the one who was driving badly, sir,' I said. 'I was going too fast on these narrow roads. Well, I can't drive that car again. This is the end of my Scottish holiday, but at least I'm not dead.'

'I'm very sorry,' he said again. He looked at his watch and continued. 'There's time to go to my house. You can change your clothes and have something to eat there. Where's your case? Is it down there in the car?'

'No. All my things are at an inn 60 kilometres away.' What could I tell him about myself? I did not want to say that I was Rhodesian. My name was in all the newspapers. The police knew that I was from Rhodesia. So I decided to be an Australian. I knew a lot about Australia. Then he could not discover who I was.

'I'm Australian,' I continued, 'and I never carry a lot of clothes with me.'

'An Australian,' he cried. 'Well, I'm the luckiest man in Scotland! You are against Protection, of course.'

'I am,' I answered quickly. But I had no idea what he meant.

'That's fine. The free movement of goods is the best thing for Britain. Well now, you'll be able to help me this evening.' He took my arm and pulled me towards his car.

A few minutes later we reached the house. He took out three or four of his suits and put them on the bed. I chose a dark blue

*I jumped out of the car and fell into the grass.*

suit and put it on. I also borrowed one of his shirts. Then he took me to the kitchen. There was some food on the table. 'If we don't hurry, we'll be late,' he said. 'Eat something now and take some food in your pocket. When we get back tonight, we'll have a good meal. We have to be in Brattleburn by seven o'clock.'

I had a cup of coffee and some cold meat. The young man stood by the fire and talked.

'You've come just at the right time, Mr – . Oh, excuse me. You haven't told me your name.'

'Twisdon,' I said.

'Ah, Twisdon. Well, I'm in trouble, Mr Twisdon, and I'd like you to help me. There's a meeting tonight at Brattleburn, and I have to make a political speech. I'm standing for Parliament for this part of Galloway, and Brattleburn is my chief town. Well, I had everything ready for the meeting, and Crumpleton – you know, the last Prime Minister – was going to make the main speech. But I had a telegram from him this afternoon. He's very ill and he can't come. That means that I have to make the speech myself.'

'Well, if you want people to vote for you,' I said, 'you should be able to make a speech.'

'Oh, I can make a short speech all right, but ten minutes is quite long enough for me. Now be a good man, Twisdon, and help me. You can tell the meeting all about the free movement of goods and Australia.'

I did not know anything about this, but I needed help too. Perhaps this was a chance.

'All right,' I said. 'I'm not a very good speaker but I'll talk to your friends about Australia.'

We left the house then and drove towards Brattleburn. On the way the young man told me a few things about himself, and one of these facts was very interesting. His father and mother were dead. So he usually lived with his uncle, who was the Chief

Secretary at the Foreign Office. This was exciting news because the Chief Secretary was an important man. I wanted to meet him. I hoped that this young man could do something for me.

We drove through a little town where two police officers stopped the car. They shone lights on our faces, and I felt very nervous. I was afraid that they were going to arrest me.

'I'm sorry, Sir Harry,' one of the officers said. 'We're looking for a stolen car.'

'Oh, that's all right.' Sir Harry laughed. 'My car is too old for anyone to steal,' he said, and we drove on.

It was five minutes to seven when we reached Brattleburn. Sir Harry stopped the car outside the town hall, and we went in. There were about 500 people in the hall. A man stood up and made a short speech. He explained that Mr Crumpleton was ill and could not come. 'But we're very lucky in Brattleburn this evening,' he continued. 'A famous speaker from Australia is here. First, though, we shall listen to the man who is going to receive every vote in Brattleburn.'

Sir Harry then began his speech. He had about 50 pages of notes in his hand and he started to read them. It was a terrible speech, and I felt very sorry for him. Sometimes he looked up from the papers, and then he lost his place. Once or twice he completely forgot where he was. He remembered a few sentences from a book and he repeated them proudly like a schoolboy. His ideas were quite wrong too. He said that the Government was making terrible mistakes; there was no danger from Germany. I almost laughed out loud.

'There's no danger from Germany at all,' he said. 'The Government has imagined it. The Germans just want to be friends, and so we don't need a big army. We're throwing away money on arms and warships.'

I thought about Scudder's little black book. The Germans' plans were ready. They were not interested in being friendly.

I spoke after Sir Harry and talked about Australia. I described the country's politics and its plans and the work of the Government there. People listened very politely and sometimes showed their agreement. But I forgot all about the free movement of goods!

The speakers were thanked at the end of the meeting. Sir Harry and I got into the car again and drove out of Brattleburn.

'That was a fine speech, Twisdon,' he said, 'and they enjoyed it. Now we'll go home and you can have a good meal. I want you to stay at my house tonight.'

After dinner that night we sat by the fire and talked.

'Listen, Sir Harry,' I said. 'I want to tell you something and it's very important. You're a good man, so I won't hide anything from you. You're quite wrong.'

He looked very surprised. 'You mean, in my speech?' he asked. 'Do you mean about the danger from Germany? Do you think they'll attack us?'

'They will probably attack us next month,' I said. 'Now listen to this story. A few days ago a German spy killed a friend of mine in London . . .'

I remember the light from the fire in Sir Harry's room. I lay back in a big chair and told him everything. I repeated all Scudder's notes and I even remembered about the 39 steps and the tide. I described my adventures with the milkman and the police at the inn.

Then I said, 'The police are trying to arrest me for the murder. But I can prove that I didn't kill Scudder. The fact is that I'm afraid of these German spies. They're much cleverer than the police. If the police arrest me, there will be an accident. And I'll get a knife in my heart, like Scudder.'

Sir Harry was looking at me thoughtfully. 'Are you a nervous man, Mr Hannay?' he asked.

I did not answer him in words. I took down a heavy knife

from the wall. I threw the knife up in the air and caught it in my mouth.

'I learned to do that many years ago in Rhodesia,' I said. 'But a nervous man couldn't do it.'

He smiled. 'All right, Hannay. You needn't prove it. I don't know much about politics but I know an honest man. I believe what you've said. Tell me what I can do to help you.'

'Well, your uncle is the Chief Secretary at the Foreign Office and he'll be able to do something. I want you to write a letter to him. Ask him if I can meet him before 15 June.'

'What name shall I say?'

'Twisdon. It's safer to forget the name Hannay.'

Sir Harry sat down at a table and wrote this letter.

*Dear Uncle,*

*I have given your address to a man named Twisdon who wants to meet you. He hopes to see you before 15 June. Be kind to him, please, and believe his story.*

*When he comes, he'll say the words "Black Stone". And he'll sing a few lines of "Annie Laurie".*

'Well, that looks all right,' Sir Harry said. 'My uncle's name is Sir Walter Bullivant, and his house is near Artinswell on the River Kennet. Now, what's the next thing?'

'Can you give me an old suit of clothes?' I said. 'And show me a map of Galloway. If the police come here to look for me, you can show them the car. But don't tell them anything.'

'And if the spies come, what shall I say to them?'

'Say that I've gone to London.'

Sir Harry brought the clothes and a map of Galloway. I looked at the map and found the railway to the south.

'That's the emptiest part of the country,' Sir Harry said, showing me an area not far away. 'Go up the road here and then turn to the right. You will be in the hills before breakfast. You'll be quite safe up there but you'll have to travel south on 12 or 13 June.'

He gave me an old bicycle and at two o'clock in the morning I left his house. At five o'clock the sun came up and I was about 30 kilometres away. Green hills rose around me on every side.

## Chapter 5   The Roadman Who Wore Glasses

I rested for a time on the top of a hill. The road ran across a flat space in front of me and then down to a river. A small house stood in the fields below, but there were no other signs of life. I was very tired, so I lay down and closed my eyes.

It was seven o'clock when a sound woke me; it was the plane again. I did not move. It flew low over the hills. It turned towards me and I could see the two men in it. Both men were looking at me. I felt sure that they knew me. Then the machine climbed quickly and flew away to the east. I had to get away from that place before they returned. They probably saw my bicycle, so I had to throw it away.

I left the road and pushed the bicycle into some trees. Then I saw a small pool and threw the bicycle into it. The day was warm and clear and I could see the road to the east and the west. There was nothing on it. But I was sure that my enemies were on their way down that road. So I turned across the hills to the north.

After a time I looked back. My eyes are very good, and I saw a line of men walking side by side. There was a space of about 9 metres between one man and the next. They were all coming towards the high ground. I ran but did not get very far. There were more men in front.

'I can't get away from here,' I thought. 'If I move, they'll see me. So I have to stay on the high ground and hide somewhere.'

*It was seven o'clock when a sound woke me; it was the plane again.*

I ran along the top of the hill and reached the road again. I turned a corner of the road and there I found the roadman. He was preparing for work, but he was moving very slowly. He looked up as I came near.

'This is a terrible job,' he said, 'and I can't do it today. I'm too ill to work, and that's a fact.'

He was a strange-looking man and he wore a pair of large glasses. His eyes looked very red.

'What's the matter?' I asked, but I knew the answer. 'You do this job every day, don't you? Why can't you do it today?'

'I do,' he replied, 'but my daughter doesn't come home from London every day. She came home yesterday, and we had a party last night.' He took off his glasses and then continued. 'I got very drunk last night and my head feels terrible.'

'I'm sorry,' I said. 'Bed is clearly the best place for you.'

'Ah, but it's not easy. My new boss is coming today to see me and my work. If I go home to bed, he won't find me here. And then I'll lose my job.'

Suddenly I had a good idea. 'Listen,' I said. 'Perhaps I can help you. Does the new boss know you very well?'

'No. I don't know him but I know about him. He travels around in a little car.'

'Where's your house?' I asked.

He showed me a small house in the fields below.

'Good. You go back to bed then and get some sleep. I'll do your job. If the boss doesn't know you, he won't know me either.'

He looked at me and then laughed. 'Well, you're a very nice man. It'll be quite easy too and you needn't do much work.'

He showed me a pile of stones. 'I broke up those stones yesterday,' he said, 'and you needn't do any more of that. Go down the road until you come to a pile of rocks. Bring them up here. I'll break them up tomorrow. My name is Alexander Turnbull but my friends call me Specky. That's because I wear these glasses. When the boss comes, you'll have to talk politely. And call him "Sir". He'll be quite happy then.'

'Perhaps the boss knows that you wear glasses,' I said. 'Let me borrow them for today.'

He laughed again. 'Well, well, this is fun.' He gave me his glasses and his dirty old hat.

I took off my coat and gave it to him. 'Take this home with you,' I said, 'and keep it for me.'

Then he left me.

Ten minutes later I looked like a roadman myself. I had put dirt on my trousers and shoes. Turnbull's trousers were tied below the knee, so I tied mine in the same way. Spies look at everything, and I was worried about my hands. They looked clean and rather soft, so I made them dirty.

Turnbull's food and an old newspaper lay on the side of the road. It was eight o'clock now, and I was feeling quite hungry. So I stole some of his bread and cheese and had a quick meal.

Then I began my new job and carried the rocks up the road. While I was working, I remembered an old friend in Rhodesia. He was a policeman when I knew him. His life was strange and difficult. When he was in danger, he often dressed as another person. He told me, 'But clothes alone aren't enough, Hannay. You have to try to *be* another person and you have to believe it yourself. If you can't do that, you will fail.'

So now I believed that I was the roadman. And I thought about my life and my job. I lived in the little house below. My daughter came home yesterday and we had a party. I got drunk and was feeling sick. But the new boss wanted to see me today, and I had to wait for him.

I worked for an hour or more and got quite dirty. It was a very dirty job. Suddenly a voice spoke from the road and I looked up. A young man was talking to me from a small car.

'Are you Alexander Turnbull?' he asked. 'I'm your new boss,

and my office is in the town hall at Newton-Stewart. The road looks all right here, Turnbull. There's a soft part about a kilometre away, and you should clean the sides of the road. I'll be around here again next week. Good morning.'

He drove away, and I felt very happy. My acting was quite good enough for him.

At about eleven o'clock a farmer drove some sheep down the road. When he saw me, he stopped.

'Where's Specky?' he asked.

'He's ill,' I replied. 'I'm doing his job for a few days.'

At about midday a big car came down the road. It went past me and stopped about a hundred metres away. Three men got out of the car and walked slowly back towards me. I knew two of them. They were the men who visited the Galloway inn. One of them was thin and dark and the other was rather fat. But I did not know the third man, who was older than the others.

'Good morning,' the third man said. 'You have a nice easy job here.'

I took my time. I put down a large rock and stood up slowly. They were watching me, and their eyes missed nothing.

'There are worse jobs than this,' I said, 'but there are probably better ones too. I'd like to have yours and sit all day in that big car.'

The elder man was now looking at Turnbull's newspaper.

'Do you get the papers every day?' he asked.

'Yes, I get them but they're three or four days late.'

He picked up the paper and looked at the date on it. Then he put it down again. The thin one was looking at my shoes and spoke a few words in German.

Then the older man said, 'You have a fine pair of shoes. Did you buy them here?'

'I did not,' I said. 'These shoes came from London. I got them from the gentleman who was shooting here last year. Now what

*Three men got out of the car and walked slowly back towards me.*

was his name?' And I tried to remember the name.

The fat man now spoke in German. 'Let's go,' he said. 'This man is all right.'

They asked me one more question. 'Did anyone go past here early this morning? Perhaps he was riding a bicycle.'

I thought about this question for a moment. Then I said, 'Well, I was a bit late this morning. My daughter came home from London yesterday and we had a party last night. I left the house at about seven o'clock, and there was nobody on the road then.'

The three men said goodbye to me and went back to their car. Three minutes later they drove away. I felt very happy, but I continued to work. It was good that I did, too; the car soon returned. The three men looked at me again as they went past.

I finished Turnbull's bread and cheese and by five o'clock the work was completed. But I was not sure about the next step. I felt sure that my enemies were staying in the area. I decided to go down to Turnbull's house. I could take his things back to him and get my coat. I could stay there until it was dark. And then I hoped to get away across the hills.

But suddenly another car came down the road and stopped. There was one man in it and he called to me.

'Have you got a light?'

I looked at him and knew him. This was a very lucky chance. His name was Marmaduke Jopley, and I saw him once or twice in London before the murder. I hated the man. He was a friend of rich young men and old ladies who often invited him to their homes. Well, Jopley was too weak to hurt me. I decided to act quickly.

'Hullo, Jopley,' I said. 'I'm surprised to see you here.'

His face grew pale. 'Who are you?' he asked in a nervous voice.

'Hannay,' I said. 'From Rhodesia. Don't you remember me?'

'Hannay the murderer!' he cried.

'That's right. Now listen to me. If you don't do this quickly, I'll be Jopley's murderer too. Give me your coat and hat.'

He was very frightened. He did what I told him to. I put on his new coat over my dirty clothes and put his hat on my head. Then I gave him Turnbull's glasses and dirty old hat.

'Wear them for a few minutes,' I said. 'Nobody will know you.'

Which way now? Jopley was driving from the east, and I decided to go back that way. I got in the car and ordered Jopley into the passenger seat. Then I drove off.

'Now, Jopley,' I said, 'if you're no trouble, I won't hurt you. But don't try anything and don't talk. Remember that I'm a murderer. If you make any trouble, I'll kill you.'

We drove 13 kilometres along the road. Several men were standing on the corners while we drove past. They looked at the car but did not try to stop us. At about seven o'clock I turned into a narrow road and drove up into the hills. The villages and houses were soon behind us. At last I stopped the car in a quiet place. I gave Jopley his coat and hat and took back Turnbull's glasses and the old hat.

'Thank you,' I said. 'Now you can go and find the police.'

I watched the red light of his car as he drove over the hill.

## Chapter 6   The Man with the Strange Eyes

It was a cold night and I was very hungry. Turnbull had my coat, and my watch and Scudder's notebook were in one of its pockets. My money was in the pocket of my trousers. I lay down in some long grass but could not sleep. I thought about all the people who were helping me. And I decided that I was a very lucky man.

Food was my main problem. I closed my eyes and saw thick

pieces of meat on a white plate. I remembered all my past meals in London. There I often refused fruit after dinner! Now an apple was just a dream.

Towards morning I slept a little, but I woke again at about six o'clock. I sat up and looked down the hill. Then I lay back down again in great surprise. Men were searching the long grass below me and they were not far away.

I moved a few feet and hid behind a rock. Then I climbed up behind the rock to the top of the hill. When I reached the top, I looked back again. My enemies were a long way below. I ran over the hill-top to the other side. Nobody could see me there, so I ran for half a kilometre. Then I climbed to the top again and looked down. The men saw me and moved towards me. I ran back over the hill-top and returned to my first hiding place. My enemies were now going the wrong way, and I felt safer.

My best plan was to go to the north, and I chose a good path. Soon there was a river between me and my enemies. But when they discovered their mistake, they turned back quickly. I saw them suddenly above the hill-top, and they began to shout at me. I saw then that they were not my real enemies. Two of them were policemen.

'Jopley has reported me,' I thought, 'and now they're looking for the murderer.'

Two men ran down and began to climb my hill. The policemen ran across the hill-tops to the north. I felt frightened now because these men knew the country. I had strong legs but did not know the best paths.

I left my hill-top and ran down towards a different river. There was a road along the side of it, and there was a gate at the side of the road. I jumped over the gate and ran across a field. The path led through a group of trees. I stopped in the trees and looked back. The police were half a kilometre behind me.

I climbed over a low wall where the trees came to an end. I

*There was a glass building at the side of the house, and an old man was sitting at a desk inside.*

found myself in a farmyard. The farmhouse was about a 30 metres away.

There was a glass building at the side of the house, and an old man was sitting at a desk inside. He looked up at me when I walked towards the building. The room was full of books and cases which contained old pieces of stone and broken pots. I saw several glass cases of old money. Books and papers covered the old man's desk.

He was a kind-looking old man with a round face and not much hair. When I entered, he did not move or speak. I could not say a word either. I looked at him and saw his eyes. They were small and clear and very intelligent. The skin on his head was smooth and shone like a glass bottle.

Then he said slowly, 'You are in a hurry, my friend.'

His eyes followed mine across the farmyard and the field. Some people were climbing over the gate at the road.

'Ah, they're policemen,' he said, 'and you're running away from them. Well, we can talk about it later. I don't want the police to come in here. If you go into the next room, you'll see two doors. Go through the doorway on the left and shut it behind you. You'll be quite safe in there.'

Then he picked up a pen and went on with his work.

I did what he said. I went into the next room and through the left-hand doorway. It was very dark inside. There was only one window, which was high up in the wall. I was safe from the police in that room but I was not very happy. Everything seemed too easy, and I began to think to myself, 'Why did that old man help me? He doesn't know me, and he didn't ask me any questions.'

While I was waiting, I thought about food again. I made plans for my breakfast, and it was very exciting. I wanted eggs. The old man could not refuse to give me some. I was ready for about ten of them. I was thinking about this meal when the door opened. A man who was standing outside made a sign to me. I followed him to the old gentleman's room.

'Have the police gone?' I asked.

'Yes. They asked me if you were here. But I didn't tell them anything important. This is a lucky morning for you, Mr Hannay.'

He spoke quietly and with the voice of a young man. I was watching him all the time. He closed his eyes but they were only half-shut, like the eyes of a bird. And I suddenly remembered Scudder's words. 'If you see his eyes, Hannay, you'll never forget them.' Was this man Scudder's worst enemy? And was I now in the enemy's house? Was it time to kill him? He guessed my plan and smiled. Then his eyes moved to the door behind me. I turned. Two large men were standing there for his protection.

He knew my name but he did not know my face. And this was my only chance.

'What are you talking about?' I asked. 'My name isn't Richard Hannay. It's Ainslie.'

'Is it? But of course you have other names. We won't fight about a name.' He continued to smile at me.

I thought of another plan quickly. I had no coat and my clothes were very dirty. So I began to tell him a story.

'Why did you save me from the police?' I asked. 'I didn't want to steal that money. It has given me a lot of trouble. You can have it.' And I took four pounds from my pocket and threw them on the old man's desk.

'Take it,' I said, 'and let me go.'

'Oh, no, Mr Hannay, I won't let you go. You know too much. You're acting very well but not well enough.'

I couldn't tell if he was sure about me.

'I am not acting,' I said. 'Why don't you believe me? I stole that money because I was hungry. The two men left the car and went away after the accident. I climbed down the bank and found the money on the floor of the car. The police are looking for me, and I'm very tired.'

The old man was clearly not sure now.

'Tell me your adventures,' he said. 'Tell me about yesterday.'

'I can't. I'm really hungry. Give me a meal first, and then I'll tell you everything.'

He made a sign to one of the men, who brought me some cold meat and a glass of milk. Suddenly, while I was eating, the old man spoke to me in German. I did not look up or answer him.

When I finished eating, I began my story again. I was on my way from Leith to visit my brother in Wigtown. I was not travelling by train because I did not have much money. On my way I saw an accident. A car ran off the road. A man jumped out of the car before it fell. And then another man came. They talked for a few moments and then went away together. I climbed down to the car. It was completely destroyed, but I found the four pounds on the floor. I put the money in my pocket and ran away.

I went into a shop in the nearest village and tried to buy some food. I offered a pound to the shopkeeper. She did not like the look of me and called the police. I got away, but the policeman tore my coat off.

'Well,' I cried, 'they can have the money back. A poor man hasn't got a chance.'

'That's a good story, Hannay,' the old man said. 'But I don't believe it.' Then he sat back in his chair and began to play with his right ear.

'It's true,' I shouted. 'My name is Ainslie, not Hannay. Those policemen knew me and were shouting my name from the hill-top.'

I looked at the clear eyes and the shining head in front of me. He was not at all sure. He did not know my face. It was different from my photographs. And my clothes were very old and dirty.

'You'll have to stay here,' he said at last. 'If you aren't Richard Hannay, you'll be quite safe. But if you *are*, I'll kill you myself.'

He pushed a bell and another man came in.

'Bring the car,' he said. 'There'll be three for dinner.'

He looked at me again, and there was something quite terrible in his eyes. They were cold and hard, and very dangerous. I could not look away from them. They made me weak, like a child, and I wanted to go to him. He was Scudder's worst enemy. But for a moment I needed to join him.

He spoke in German to one of the men. And when I heard his words, my strange thoughts left me.

'Karl, put him in the back room and don't let him get away. Remember that,' he said.

The room was very dark, but the two men did not come inside with me. They sat down outside, where I could hear them talking. I felt around the walls of the room and touched several boxes. Then I sat down on one of the boxes to think about my problems.

The old man's friends *did* know my face. They knew me as the roadman, and I was wearing Turnbull's clothes. I could imagine their questions: Why were the police looking for a roadman? Why was he found 30 kilometres away from his job? They probably remembered Marmaduke Jopley too, I thought, and Sir Harry. I could not continue to lie to these foreign enemies and I did not want to be alone with them here. My chances of getting away were not very great.

Suddenly I grew angry and hated these German spies in Britain. I could not sit in this dark place and do nothing. I had to attack them or try to get away.

I got up and walked around the room again. The boxes were too strong for me to open, but then I found a cupboard in the wall. It was probably locked, because I could not open it. But there was a hole in the door. I pushed my fingers into the hole and then pulled hard. The door of the cupboard broke open.

There were some strange things inside. There were bottles and small boxes and some old yellow bags. I found a box of detonators. I took out the detonators and placed them on the floor. At the back of the cupboard I found a strong box. At first I thought that it was locked. But it opened quite easily, and it was full of sticks of dynamite.

I could destroy the house with this dynamite. I often used it in Rhodesia and I knew it well. It could very easily destroy me too! This was clearly a chance to get away, and it was probably my only chance. So I decided to take it.

I found a hole in the floor near the doorway. I pushed a stick of dynamite into the hole and tied a detonator and a long piece of cotton to it. Then I moved one of the boxes until it stood over the hole. I sat down near the cupboard and lit the piece of cotton. I watched the fire as it moved along the cotton. The two men were talking quietly outside the door.

Suddenly there was a terrible noise, and great heat and light came up from the floor. They hung for a moment in the air, and then clouds of dirt took their place. Thick yellow smoke filled the room, and at first I could not see anything. But there was light in the room now from a great hole in the wall. I ran towards it. The air outside was also full of smoke, and I could hear the sound of voices.

I climbed through the hole and ran. I was in the farmyard at the back of the house. About 30 metres away there was a tall stone bird-house. The building had no doors or windows but there were a lot of small holes for the birds. And the roof seemed flat. It looked a good place to hide.

I ran through the smoke to the back of the bird-house. Then I began to climb. It was hard work, and I went up very slowly. But at last I reached the top and lay down behind a low wall. I felt sick from the smoke and very tired. But I was safe up there and soon I fell asleep.

I probably slept for several hours. When I woke up, the

*I climbed through the hole and ran.*

afternoon sun was very strong. I could hear men's voices again and the sound of a car. I lifted my head a little and looked over the wall. Four or five men were walking across the farmyard to the house. The old man was with them and he was clearly very angry. He shouted something in German to the other men. The thin dark one was there, and the fat one too.

I lay on the roof of the bird-house all afternoon. I was very thirsty. There was a little river next to the farm and I could hear the sound of water. I felt the money in my pocket. Almost no price was too high for a glass of water at that moment!

Two men drove away in the car. A little later another man rode towards the east on a horse. The search was beginning, but they were all going the wrong way. I sat up on the roof and looked around. At first I saw nothing very interesting but then my eyes fell on a large area of trees. These trees were half a kilometre from the house, and they stood around a flat green field.

'That looks like an airfield,' I thought. 'It's a good place for a secret airfield.'

You could not see the field from the ground and a small plane could land there between the trees.

Then I saw a thin blue line far away to the south. It was the sea. So our enemies had this secret airfield in Scotland, and they could watch our ships every day. The thought made me very angry. It made me nervous too. Someone in a plane could easily see me below them. But I could do nothing until it was dark.

I lay and waited on the roof of the bird-house. At about six o'clock a man came out through the hole in my prison. He walked slowly towards the bird-house, and I felt quite frightened for a moment. But then we both heard the plane at the same time. The man turned and went back inside.

The plane did not fly over the house, and I was happy about that. It flew around the trees once and then landed. Some lights shone for a moment or two, and ten minutes later I heard voices.

After that everything was quiet, and it began to grow dark.

I waited until about nine o'clock. Then I climbed down from the roof and reached the ground safely. I moved away from the bird-house on my hands and knees. I went first to the little river. I lay there and drank the cold water. Then I began to run. I wanted to get as far away as possible from that terrible house.

## Chapter 7   The Fisherman

I was free now but I felt rather sick. I could smell the smoke of the dynamite and an hour later I had to rest.

It was about 11 o'clock when I reached the road safely. I wanted to go back to Mr Turnbull's cottage. My coat was there, with Scudder's notebook in the pocket, and I had to have that book. My plan then was to find the railway and travel to the south. After that I hoped to go straight to Artinswell to meet Sir Walter Bullivant.

It was a beautiful night. I knew that Turnbull's cottage was about 30 kilometres away. It was too far for me to walk before morning. So I decided to hide during the day and travel only at night.

When the sun rose, I was near a river. I washed in the clean cold water because I was very dirty. My shirt and trousers were torn, and I was afraid to meet anyone in that state. But just the other side of the river I came to a cottage. And I was so hungry that I had to stop there.

The man was not at home, and at first his wife did not like the look of me. She picked up a stick and seemed ready to attack me.

'I've had a bad fall in the hills,' I said, 'and I'm feeling ill. Will you help me?'

She did not ask any questions but invited me into the house. She gave me a glass of milk and some bread and cheese. Then I sat by the fire in her kitchen and we talked. I offered her money for her trouble, but she refused it at first.

'If it isn't your money, I don't want it,' she said.

I grew quite angry. 'But it *is* my money. Do you think that I stole it?'

She accepted it then and unlocked a cupboard in the wall. She gave me a warm piece of Scottish cloth to put over my shoulder and one of her husband's hats. When I left her cottage, I was like a real Scotsman!

I walked for two or three hours. Then the weather changed and it began to rain. But I kept warm and dry under the cloth. A little later I came to a large rock which hung over some low ground. The grass under the rock was quite dry. So I lay down and slept there all day.

When I woke up, it was almost dark. The weather was the same, wet and cold, and I was not sure of the way. Twice I took the wrong path and probably walked more than 30 kilometres. But at six o'clock in the morning I reached Mr Turnbull's cottage.

Mr Turnbull opened the door himself, but he did not know me. 'Who are you?' he asked. 'Why are you coming here on a Sunday morning? I'm just getting ready to go to church.'

I knew nothing about the days of the week; every day seemed the same to me. I felt too ill to answer him. But then he remembered me.

'Have you got my glasses?' he asked.

I took them out of my pocket and gave them to him.

'Of course, you've come back for your coat,' he said. 'Come in, man. You look terrible. Wait. I'll get you a chair.'

When I was in Rhodesia, I was often ill. And one of these African illnesses returned time after time. I knew the signs very well. Soon Mr Turnbull was taking off my clothes and leading me to a bed.

I stayed with him for ten days, and he looked after me very well. The illness lasted about six days. Then my body returned to its usual temperature and I got up.

He went out to work every morning and returned in the evening. I rested all day. He had a cow which gave us milk. And there was always some food in the house.

One evening I said, 'There's a small airfield about 24 kilometres away. Do you know it? A little plane lands there sometimes. Who owns the place?'

'I don't know,' he said. 'I've seen the plane, of course, but I don't know anything about it.'

He brought me several newspapers while I was staying with him. I read them with interest, but I saw nothing about the murder in London. Turnbull did not ask me any questions, not even my name. I was surprised about this, and one day I said, 'Has anyone asked you about me?'

'There was a man in a car,' he said. 'He stopped one day and asked me about the other roadman. That was you, of course. He seemed a very strange man, so I didn't tell him anything.'

When I left the cottage, I gave Turnbull five pounds. He did not want to take the money at all. His face grew red, and he was quite rude to me. 'I don't want money,' he said. 'When I was ill, you helped me. Then you were ill, and I helped you. I can't take such a lot of money.' But he took it in the end.

The weather was beautiful that morning, but I was beginning to feel nervous. It was 12 June, and I had to finish Scudder's business before the 15th. I had dinner at a quiet inn in Moffat and then went to the railway station. It was seven o'clock in the evening.

'What time does the train go to London?' I asked.

'Ten minutes to twelve,' the railway man said.

It was a long time to wait, so I left the station. I found a quiet place near a hill-top and lay down there to sleep. I was so tired that I slept until twenty minutes to twelve. Then I ran down to the station where the train was waiting.

I decided not to go to London. I got out of the train at Crewe and waited there for two hours. The next train took me to Birmingham, and I reached Reading at six o'clock in the evening. Two hours later I was looking for Sir Walter Bullivant's cottage at Artinswell.

The River Kennet ran along next to the road. The English air was sweet and warm, quite different from Scottish air. I stood for a few minutes on a bridge which went across the river. And I began to sing "Annie Laurie" in a low voice.

A fisherman came up from the bank of the river. As he walked towards me, he began to sing "Annie Laurie" too.

The fisherman was a great big man. He was wearing an old pair of grey trousers and a large hat. He looked at me and smiled. And I thought that he had a good and honest face. Then he looked down with me at the water.

'It's clean and clear, isn't it?' he said. 'The Kennet's a fine river. Look at that big fish down there. But the sun has gone now. If you try all night, you won't catch him.'

'Where?' I said. 'I can't see him.'

'Look. Down there. A metre from those water plants.'

'Oh, yes. I can see him now. He's like a big *black stone*, isn't he?'

'Ah,' he said, and sang a few more words of "Annie Laurie".

He continued to look down at the water. 'Your name is Twisdon, I believe,' he said.

'No,' I said. Then I remembered my other names and added quickly, 'Oh, yes, that's right.'

He laughed. 'A good spy always knows his own name,' he said.

Some men were walking across the bridge behind us, and Sir Walter spoke more loudly.

'No, I won't,' he said. 'You're strong enough to work, aren't

*I stood for a few minutes on a bridge which went across the river. And I began to sing "Annie Laurie" in a low voice.*

you? You can get a meal from my kitchen, but I won't give you any money.'

The men went past, and the fisherman moved away from me. He showed me to a white gate a hundred metres away and said, 'That's my house. Wait here for five minutes and then go around to the back door.'

When I reached his cottage, the back door was open. Sir Walter's butler was waiting to welcome me.

'Come this way, sir,' he said, and he led me up the stairs. He took me into one of the bedrooms. There were clothes on the bed. I saw a dinner-suit and a clean white shirt. But there were other clothes too and several pairs of shoes.

'I hope that these things will fit you, sir,' the butler said. 'Your bath is ready in the next room. You'll hear the bell for dinner at nine o'clock, sir.'

When he left, I sat down. I thought that I was dreaming. At this time the day before I was asleep on a Scottish hill-top. Now I was in this beautiful house, and Sir Walter did not even know my name.

I had a bath and then put on the white shirt and the dinner-suit. Everything fitted me very well. The bell went for dinner, and I hurried down to meet Sir Walter.

'You're very kind, sir,' I said, 'but it is time to tell you about my situation. I haven't done anything wrong, but the police are looking for me at this moment.'

He smiled. 'That's all right. We can talk about these things after dinner. I'm pleased that you got here safely.'

I enjoyed that meal, and the wine was good too. Sir Walter was an interesting man who had travelled in many foreign countries. I talked about Rhodesia and the fish in the Zambesi River, and he told me some of his adventures.

After dinner we went into his library, and the butler brought us coffee. It was a very nice room, with books and fine pictures around the walls. I decided to buy a house like that after I finished Scudder's work.

Sir Walter lay back in his chair.

'I've followed Harry's orders,' he said. 'And now I'm ready to listen, Mr Hannay. You've got some news, I believe.'

I was surprised to hear my real name, but I began my story. And I told him everything. I described my meeting with Scudder and his fears about Karolides. I told him about the murder and my adventure with the milkman.

'Where did you go then?' he asked.

'I went to Galloway. I soon discovered the secret of Scudder's code and then I could read his notes.'

'Have you got them with you?'

'Yes.'

Then I described my meeting with Sir Harry and how I helped him at Brattleburn.

Sir Walter laughed. 'Harry can't make a speech,' he said. 'He's a good man but his ideas are very strange. Please go on with your story, Mr Hannay.'

I told him about Turnbull then and my job as a roadman. He was very interested in that.

'Can you describe those men in the car?' he asked.

'Well, one of them was thin and dark. I saw him before at the inn with the fat one. But I didn't know the third man, who was older than the others.'

'And what did you do after that?'

'I met Marmaduke Jopley next, and had a bit of fun with him.' Sir Walter laughed again when I described that part of the story. But he did not laugh at the old man in the farmhouse.

'How did you get away from the place?' he asked.

'I found dynamite and detonators in a cupboard,' I replied, 'and I almost destroyed the building. There's a small airfield there where the plane lands. After that I was ill for a week. Turnbull looked after me very well. Then I travelled south by train, and here I am.'

Sir Walter stood up slowly and looked down at me.

'You needn't be afraid of the police, Hannay,' he said. 'They aren't looking for you now.'

I was surprised to hear this.

'Why?' I cried. 'Have they found the murderer?'

'No, not yet. But the police know that you didn't kill Scudder.'

'How do they know that?'

'Because I received a letter from Scudder. He did several jobs for me, and I knew him quite well. He was a good spy, but he had one problem.'

'What was that?'

'He always wanted to work alone, and he failed for that reason. The best spies always work with others, but Scudder couldn't do that. I was very sorry about it because he was a fine man. I had a letter from him on 31 May.'

'But he was dead then. He was killed on 23 May, wasn't he?'

'Yes, and he wrote the letter on the 23rd. He sent the letter to Spain first, and then it came back to England.'

'What did he write about?'

'He told me that Britain was in great danger. He also said that he was staying with a good friend. And I believe that the "good friend" was you, Hannay. He promised to write again soon.'

'What did you do then?'

'I went to the police. They knew your name and we sent a telegram to Rhodesia. The answer was all right, so we were not worried about you. I guessed why you left London. You wanted to continue Scudder's work, didn't you? Then I got Harry's letter and I guessed that Twisdon was Richard Hannay.'

I was very pleased to hear all this. My country's enemies were my enemies, but the police were now my friends. And I was a free man again!'

Sir Walter sat down and smiled at me.

'Show me Scudder's notes,' he said.

I took out the little book and began to explain the code to him. He was very quick and he knew what the names meant. We worked hard for an hour or more.

'Scudder was right about one thing,' he said. 'A French officer is coming to London on 15 June, and that's the day after tomorrow. I thought that it was all secret. Of course we know that there are a few German spies in England. We've got some of our men in Germany too. But how did they all discover the secret of this Frenchman's visit? I don't believe Scudder's story about war and the Black Stone. He always had some strange ideas.'

Sir Walter stood up again and walked about the room. 'The Black Stone,' he repeated. '*Der Schwarzestein*. It's like something out of a cheap story, isn't it? I don't believe the part about Karolides either. He's an important man, but nobody wants to kill him. Perhaps Scudder heard about some danger, but it isn't very important. It's the usual spy business, which the Germans enjoy very much. Sometimes they kill a man in the way that they killed Scudder. And the German government pays them for it.'

The butler came into the room.

'It's the telephone, sir,' he said. 'Your office in London. Mr Heath wants to speak to you.'

Sir Walter left the library. When he returned a few minutes later, he looked quite pale.

'Scudder was right,' he said, 'and I was wrong. Karolides is dead. He was shot about three hours ago.'

## Chapter 8    The Black Stone

In the morning the butler took away the dinner-suit and gave me some other clothes. I went down to breakfast and found Sir Walter at the table. There was a telegram in his hand.

'I was busy last night,' he said. 'I spoke to the Foreign Secretary and to the Secretary for War. They telephoned the First Lord of the Admiralty, and they're bringing the Frenchman to London today, not tomorrow. His name's Royer, and he'll be here at five o'clock this evening. This telegram is from the First Lord of the Admiralty.'

He offered me the hot food on the table, and I began to eat. It was a very good breakfast.

'I don't think that this change is going to help us,' he continued. 'Our enemies discovered the first date, so they'll probably discover the new one too. There has to be a German spy in the Foreign Office or in the War Office. Only five men knew that Royer was coming. That's what we believed, at least. But someone told Scudder and the Germans.'

'Can't you change your plans for war?' I asked.

'We can but we don't want to. We've thought a lot about these plans and they're the best possible ones.'

'But if it's necessary, you will change them.'

'Perhaps. It's a difficult problem, Hannay. Our enemies aren't children. They're not going to steal any papers from Royer. They want to know our plans, but they want to get them in secret. Then Royer will go back to France and say, "Here are the British plans for war, and they're completely secret. The Germans don't know anything about them."'

'Then you'll have to give the Frenchman special protection,' I said. 'Someone who will stay by his side all the time.'

'Royer is having dinner with the Foreign Secretary tonight. Then he's coming to my house, where he'll meet four people.

They are Sir Arthur Drew, General Winstanley, Mr Whittaker and me. The First Lord isn't well, so Whittaker is coming in his place. And he's bringing the plans from the First Lord's office at the Admiralty. We'll take them to Royer, who will then leave for Portsmouth. A warship is waiting there to take him to France. He'll have special protection all the time.'

After breakfast we left for London by car.

Sir Walter said, 'I'm taking you to Scotland Yard, Hannay. I want you to meet the Chief of Police.'

It was half past eleven when we reached Scotland Yard. We walked into the great dark building, and I met the Chief of Police. His name was MacGillivray.

'I've brought you the murderer,' Sir Walter said.

The Chief smiled. 'I'll be very happy when you bring me the real murderer, Bullivant. Good morning, Mr Hannay. You interest us greatly.'

'And he's going to tell you some interesting things,' Sir Walter said, 'but not today. You have to wait for 24 hours, I'm afraid. Mr Hannay is a free man now, isn't he?'

'Yes, of course,' the Chief of Police said. Then he turned to me. 'Do you want to go back to your old flat? It's ready for you, but perhaps you'd like to move to a different home.'

I was thinking about Scudder and could not reply.

'Well,' Sir Walter said, 'I have to go now. Perhaps we'll need some of your men, MacGillivray, tonight or tomorrow. There will probably be some trouble.'

When we were leaving, Sir Walter took my hand.

'You're all right now, Hannay,' he said. 'You'll be quite safe in London. Come and see me tomorrow. But don't talk about these spies, will you? It's best to stay in your flat today.' He laughed suddenly. 'If these Black Stone people see you, they'll kill you.'

When Sir Walter had left, I felt quite alone. I was a free man, and everything was all right. But I was very nervous. I went to the Savoy Hotel and ordered a fine meal. But I did not enjoy it. People were looking at me, and I thought, 'Do they know me? Did they see my photograph in the newspapers?' I soon left the hotel.

In the afternoon I got a taxi and drove several kilometres to North London. I paid the taxi-driver and then began to walk back. I walked for hours and at last came to the centre of London again. I was feeling very unhappy. It was six o'clock, and important things were taking place in London. Royer was already there. Sir Walter was busy at the Foreign Office or making plans for the meeting. The Black Stone spies were watching and waiting quietly. But what was I doing? I was walking around the centre of London.

Suddenly a strange thought came into my head. I believed that there was great danger in London that day. And I was suddenly sure that only I could fight against it. But what could I do? Sir Walter did not need me. I could not walk into a meeting of important officers and Ministers. I could look for the German spies, of course. I was quite sure of one thing: my country needed me in this time of trouble. I had to destroy their plans; the German spies must not win.

'But is that true, Hannay?' I said to myself. 'Can't Sir Walter and his friends easily look after Britain? Doesn't the First Lord of the Admiralty know his business better than you do? Can a few German spies do anything against all of them?'

I was not sure. There was a little voice in my ear which repeated again and again: 'Do something, Hannay. Get up and do something now. If you don't, you'll never sleep well again.'

At half past nine I was walking along Jermyn Street. And I decided what to do. I decided to go to Sir Walter's house. I knew the address and I could easily find it. He did not want to see me, but I had to do something.

I came to Duke Street and walked past a group of young men.

They were wearing dinner-suits and were leaving a hotel. One of the young men was Mr Marmaduke Jopley. He saw me.

'Look!' he cried. 'It's the murderer! Hold him! Hold him! That's Hannay the murderer!'

Jopley caught my arm, and the others hurried to help him. A policeman ran across the street. I hit Jopley hard with my left hand and saw him fall. But then the crowd held me and I could not move.

'What's the matter here?' the policeman said.

'That's Hannay, the murderer,' Jopley shouted.

'Oh, be quiet,' I said. 'I'm not a murderer. Listen, officer. Don't arrest me. The Chief of Police knows all about me. I was at Scotland Yard this morning.'

'Now young man, come along with me,' the policeman said. 'I saw you begin this fight.' He looked at Jopley, who was lying on the ground. 'That man didn't do anything to you, but I saw you hit him. Now come along quietly to the police station.'

I was very angry. I heard the little voice in my ear again. 'You have to get away,' it said. 'Don't spend another minute here.'

Suddenly I felt very strong. I turned quickly and threw the policeman to the ground. I pushed the other men away and ran along Duke Street.

I can run very fast when I want to. And that evening I almost flew. In a few minutes I reached Pall Mall and turned towards St James's Park. I ran between the taxis in the Mall and across the bridge. There were very few people in the park and nobody stopped me. Sir Walter's house was at Queen Anne's Gate and there I began to walk.

Three or four cars were standing in the street outside the house. I walked up to the door and pushed the bell. The butler opened the door. I could hear cries far away, but the street was empty.

'I have to see Sir Walter,' I said. 'My business is very important.'

*I hit Jopley hard with my left hand and saw him fall.*

'Come in, sir,' he said. 'I'm afraid you can't see him now. But you can wait in the hall until the meeting finishes.'

It was an old house with a large square hall. Doors led into several rooms on each side. An officer who was dressed in plain clothes stood outside one of the doors. I sat down in a corner near the telephone.

I made a sign to the butler. 'I'm in trouble again,' I said. 'But I'm working for Sir Walter, and he knows all about it. The police and a crowd of people are following me. If they come here, please don't let them come in. And don't tell them that I'm here.'

'All right, sir,' he replied.

A minute or two later I heard voices outside. Then came the sound of the door-bell, and the butler went to answer it. Someone spoke to him from outside, and he suddenly stood up very straight.

'I am sorry,' he said. 'This is Sir Walter Bullivant's house, and Sir Walter is Chief Secretary at the Foreign Office. I'm afraid that I don't know anything about a murderer. Now please go away, or I shall call the police myself.'

Then he shut the door and walked back through the hall.

Two minutes later I heard the bell again, and a man came in. While he was taking off his coat, I saw his face. It was a famous face, and I knew it from his photographs in the newspapers. The man was Lord Alloa, the First Lord of the Admiralty. He was a big man with a large nose and sharp blue eyes. He walked past me, and the plain clothes officer opened the door of the room for him.

I waited in the hall for 20 minutes. And during this time the little voice continued to speak in my ear. 'Don't go away,' it said. 'They'll soon need you.' A little bell went at the back of the house and the butler came into the hall. The First Lord left the meeting room, and the butler gave him his coat. I looked at the man for a moment, and he looked straight at me. It was all very

*I looked at the man for a moment, and he looked straight at me.*

fast. My heart jumped suddenly because I saw a light in his eyes. I did not know the First Lord, and he did not know me. But I was quite sure about that sudden light in his eyes. It meant that he knew my face. He looked away and walked to the door. The butler opened it for him and closed it behind him.

I picked up the telephone book and quickly found Lord Alloa's number. His butler answered.

'Is the First Lord at home?' I asked.

'Yes, sir,' the voice said. 'But he's not very well. He's in bed. Can I give him a message, sir?'

'No, thank you,' I said, and I put the telephone down.

I walked quickly across the hall and entered the meeting room. Five surprised faces looked up from a round table. Sir Walter was there and Drew, the War Minister. Sir Arthur Drew's photograph was often in the papers. I already knew General Winstanley. An older man, who was probably Whittaker, stood next to him. The fifth man was short and fat.

Sir Walter looked quite angry.

'This is Mr Hannay,' he said. 'I've already told you something about him. But why have you come here, Hannay? You know that we're very busy.'

'Your enemies are busy too, sir,' I said. 'And one of them has just left this room.'

Sir Walter's face grew red as he said, 'But that was Lord Alloa.'

'It was not,' I cried. 'Lord Alloa is at home in bed. I have just spoken to his butler on the telephone. The man who was here knew my face. And Lord Alloa doesn't know me.'

'Then – who – who–?' someone asked.

'The Black Stone,' I cried. I looked around the table and saw fear in five pairs of eyes.

## Chapter 9   The Thirty-Nine Steps

'But that can't be true,' Mr Whittaker said. 'Lord Alloa told me that he was probably not going to come to the meeting. But I know him very well and was not surprised to see him here. You're quite wrong about this, Hannay.'

Sir Walter left the room and spoke to someone on the telephone. When he came back, his face had turned pale.

'I've spoken to Alloa,' he said. 'He got out of bed to come to the telephone. Hannay is right. That man was not Lord Alloa.'

'I don't believe it,' General Winstanley said. 'Alloa was standing next to me ten minutes ago.'

'Gentlemen,' I said, 'the Black Stone knows its business. You probably didn't look at the man very well. You were talking about these important plans. The man looked like Lord Alloa, and so you accepted him. But it was another man, and I probably saw him in Scotland.'

Then the Frenchman spoke. 'This young man is right,' he said slowly. 'Our enemies know their business very well. Listen and I'll tell you a true story. Many years ago, I was in Senegal. I was living in a hotel but every day I went fishing. The river was a few kilometres away and I rode there on a little horse.

'Well, one day I packed my lunch as usual and hung it over the horse's neck. Then I left for the river. When I arrived there, I tied the horse to a tree. I fished for several hours, and I was thinking only about the fish. I didn't look at the horse at all, but I could hear her. And I could see her shape out of the corner of my eye. She was moving about a lot and making a bit of noise too. I spoke to her as usual, but I did not look up from the water.

'Well, lunchtime came, so I put the fish into a bag and walked along the river bank. While I was walking, I continued to watch the water. When I reached the tree, I threw the bag on to the horse's back . . .'

The Frenchman stopped and looked around the table.

'It was the smell that hit me first. I looked up and turned my head. My bag was lying on a lion's back. The horse was dead and half eaten on the ground behind him.'

'What did you do?' I asked. I knew that this was a real African story.

'I shot the lion in the head,' he said. 'But before he died, he took a part of me.' And he held up his left hand, which only had two fingers on it.

'That horse died hours before I finished fishing,' he continued. 'And the lion was watching me all the time. He was a brown shape near the tree. I saw the shape and colour but I did not really look at him. That was my mistake, gentlemen, and we have made the same mistake tonight.'

Sir Walter agreed.

'This Black Stone man,' the General said, 'is he a German spy or something? Nobody could keep all these facts in his head. It doesn't seem very important to me.'

'Oh, yes, he could,' the Frenchman replied. 'A good spy can remember everything. His eyes are like a camera. Do you remember that he didn't speak at all? He read the papers several times but didn't say anything. You can be sure that he has all the facts now. When I was young, I could do the same thing.'

'Well, we'll have to change the plans,' Sir Walter said.

Mr Whittaker looked surprised. 'Did you say that to Lord Alloa?' he asked.

'No.'

'Of course we can't decide it now. But I'm almost sure about this: if we change the plans, we'll have to change the coast of England too!'

'And there's another problem,' Royer said. 'I've told you some of the French plans, and that German spy heard them. Now we can't possibly change our plans. But we *can* do this, gentlemen:

we can catch them before they leave the country.'

'But how?' I cried. 'We don't know anything about them.'

'And there's the post,' Whittaker said. 'They can easily send the facts to Germany by post. Perhaps they are on their way there now. We can't possibly search the post.'

'No,' the Frenchman said. 'You don't know how a good spy works. He carries the secrets himself. The Germans will pay the man who brings the plans. So we have a chance. The man has to get across the sea to reach Germany, and we'll have to search all ships. Believe me, gentlemen. This matter is very important for both France and Britain.'

Royer was clearly an intelligent man, and he had the right ideas. But where could we find these German spies? The problem was a very difficult one. Then I remembered Scudder's book.

'Sir Walter,' I cried, 'did you bring Scudder's notebook from the cottage? I've just remembered something in it.'

He went to a cupboard. And a few moments later I found the page.

'*Thirty-nine steps,*' I read. '*Thirty-nine steps. I counted them. High tide is at 10.17 p.m.*'

Whittaker was looking at me. 'What does all that mean?' he asked.

'Scudder knew these spies,' I said. 'And he knew the place where they lived. They're probably leaving the country tomorrow. And I believe that we'll find them near the sea. There are steps at this place, and it has a high tide at seventeen minutes past ten.'

'But they will probably leave tonight,' someone said. 'They won't wait until tomorrow.'

'I don't think so. They have their own secret way and they're not going to hurry. They're Germans, aren't they? And Germans always like to follow a plan. Now where can we find a book of tides?'

'Well, it's a chance,' Whittaker said, 'and it's probably our only chance to catch them.'

'Isn't there a book of tides at the Admiralty?' Sir Walter asked.

'Yes, of course,' Whittaker replied. 'Let's go there now.'

We went out into the hall, and the butler gave the gentlemen their coats. We got into two of the cars, but Sir Walter did not come with us.

'I'm going to Scotland Yard,' he said. 'We'll probably need some of MacGillivray's men.'

We reached the Admiralty and followed Whittaker through several empty rooms to the map room. There he found a book of tides and gave it to me. I sat down at a desk and the others stood around me. But the job was too difficult for any of us. There were hundreds of names in the book. And high tide was at seventeen minutes past ten in forty or fifty places.

I put down the book and began to think about the steps.

'We're looking for a place,' I said, 'which probably has several staircases. But the important one has 39 steps.'

'And the tide is important too,' Royer said. 'So that means that it's probably a small port. These people won't try to get away in a big boat. They may have a small sailing boat or a fishing boat.'

'That's quite possible,' I said. 'The place may not be a port at all. These spies were in London, and now they want to go to Germany. So they'll probably leave from a place on the East Coast.'

I picked up a piece of paper and wrote down our ideas.

1. The place has several staircases. The important one has 39 steps.
2. High tide is at seventeen minutes past ten. High tide is necessary for the boat to leave.
3. The place is a small port or perhaps a piece of open coast.
4. The Germans may use a sailing boat or a fishing boat.

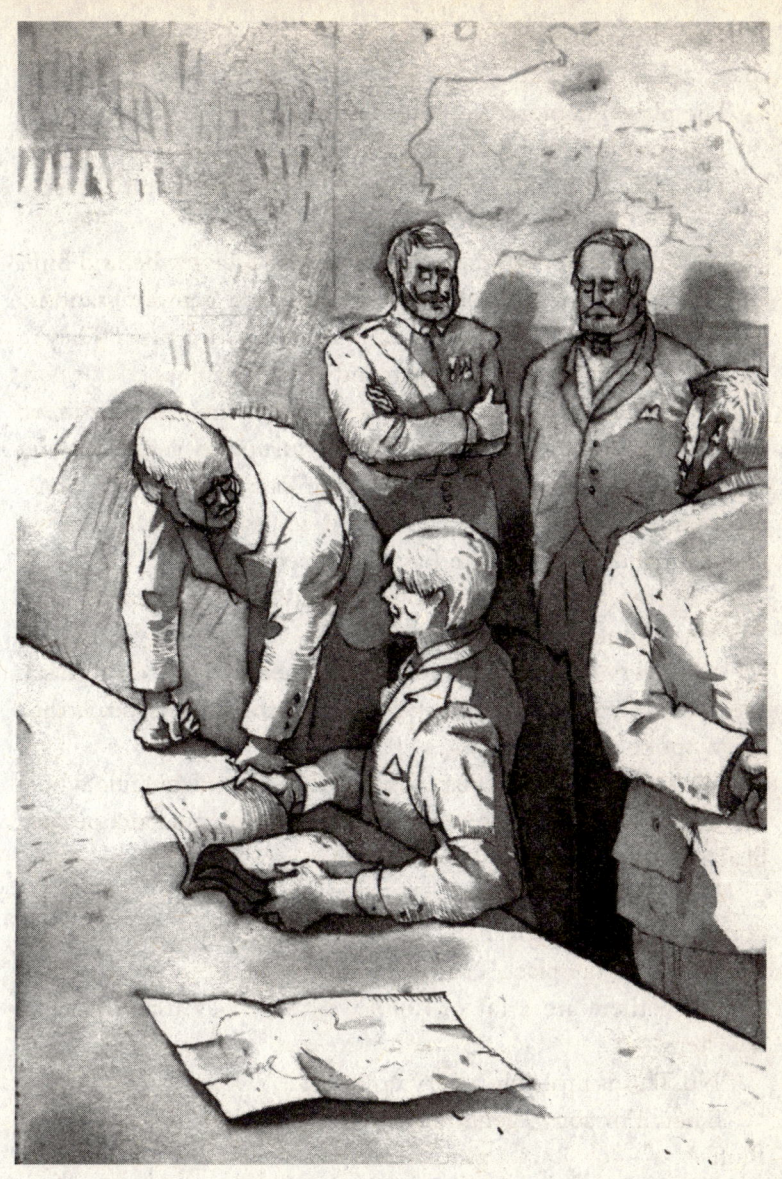

*I sat down at a desk and the others stood around me.*

Then I made three guesses and wrote them down:

1 The place is a piece of open coast.
2 The boat is probably small and foreign.
3 The place is on the East Coast between Cromer and Dover.

Sir Walter came into the room with MacGillivray behind him.

'The police are watching the ports and railway stations,' MacGillivray said. 'But it's not going to be easy for them. They're looking for a fat man, a thin man and an old man!'

I showed my paper to Sir Walter and said, 'These are our ideas. But we'll need someone to help us.' I turned to Whittaker and said, 'Is there a Chief Coastguard on the East Coast?'

'I don't know. But I know one in London. He lives in Clapham and he knows the East Coast very well.'

'Can you bring him here tonight?' I asked.

'Yes, I think so. I'll go to his house.'

It was very late when Whittaker returned with the coastguard. He was a fine old man and very polite to the officers. Sir Arthur Drew spoke to him first.

'We're looking for a place on the East Coast,' he said, 'where there are several staircases. The steps probably lead down to a beach. Do you know any place like that?'

'Well, sir, I don't know. There's Brattlesham in Norfolk, of course. There are steps there, but only the fishermen use them.'

'That isn't the place,' I said.

'Then there are a lot of holiday places. They usually have a few steps.'

'No. This is probably a very quiet place.'

'Then I'm sorry, gentlemen. I don't know. There's only the Ruff—'

'What's that?' I asked.

'It's a bit of high ground on the Kent coast. Near Bradgate.

There are some fine houses on the top and some of them have steps down to the beach. They're private beaches, of course.'

'What do you mean by that?'

'Well, the people who own the houses also own the beaches, sir. When you buy a house there, you get a piece of private beach as well.'

I picked up the book of tides and found Bradgate. High tide there was at twenty-seven minutes past ten on 15 June.

'How can I find the time of high tide at the Ruff?' I asked the coastguard.

'Oh, I know that, sir. I stayed there once in June. It's ten minutes before high tide at Bradgate.'

I shut the book and looked around.

'Sir Walter,' I said, 'can I borrow your car and a map of the roads in Kent? I'd like to have some of your men too, MacGillivray. Perhaps we can surprise these Germans tomorrow morning.'

They did not answer me for a moment. I did not work for the Foreign Office or the Admiralty, or the General. But I was young and strong and I already knew these spies.

It was Royer who spoke first. 'I'm quite happy,' he said, 'to leave this matter in Mr Hannay's hands.'

Sir Walter said, 'I think so too.' And MacGillivray agreed.

Half an hour later I was driving quickly through the villages of Kent. MacGillivray's best officer was sitting next to me in the car. It was half past three in the morning.

## Chapter 10   The House by the Sea

We stayed at the Griffin Hotel in Bradgate. At seven o'clock in the morning I was looking out of a window there. It was a beautiful day. A man was fishing down at the port, and I remembered Royer's story about the lion.

A small warship was lying south of the port. I called MacGillivray's man.

'Officer,' I said, 'do you know that ship? Perhaps Whittaker sent her here.'

'I don't think so,' he said. 'She's usually along this part of the coast.' And he told me her name and the name of her captain. I went to the telephone and sent a telegram to Sir Walter about them.

After breakfast Scaife, MacGillivray's officer, and I walked along the beach. We went towards the steps on the Ruff but stopped less than half a kilometre from them.

'I won't come all the way with you,' I said. 'These people know me very well. I'll wait here. You go on and count all the steps.'

I sat down behind a rock and waited. There was nobody on the beach. It was ten o'clock when Scaife came back.

'There are six lots of steps,' he said, 'and they lead to six different houses.' He took a piece of paper from his pocket and read: 'Thirty-four, thirty-five, thirty-nine, forty-two, forty-seven and twenty-one.'

I felt so pleased that I almost got up and shouted.

We hurried back to Bradgate and sent a telegram to MacGillivray. I wanted six good men, and they had to stay at different hotels in the town.

'Now go back to the 39 steps,' I said to Scaife, 'and have a look at the house. Then go to the post office. Find out who lives there.'

He brought back some strange but interesting facts. The house was called Trafalgar Lodge and it belonged to an old man named Appleton. Mr. Appleton often stayed there in the summer. He was at the house now. Nobody knew a lot about him but he seemed kind and quiet. Scaife made some excuse to visit the house and met three women there.

'They look after the place,' he said, 'and they can't possibly be Germans. They talk too much for that.'

'Did you look at the houses on each side of Trafalgar Lodge?' I asked.

'Yes. The house on the right is empty. They're building the place on the left.'

Before dinner I walked along the Ruff myself. I found a quiet place away from the houses and sat down there. I could see the house quite well. It was a red stone building with large windows. There was a garden all around the house, and the British flag was flying from a tall post!

While I was watching, a man left the house to walk along the hill-top. He was an old man wearing white trousers and a blue coat. He had a newspaper under his arm. He walked quite a long way and then sat down on a seat to read the paper. A few minutes later he put down the paper and looked out to sea at the warship. He looked at it for a long time. I watched him for half an hour, and then he got up to return to the house. I went back to my hotel.

I was not very happy about that old man. He did not look like a spy, but perhaps he was the old man from that Scottish farm.

In the afternoon we had some excitement. A sailing boat came up from the south and stopped near the Ruff. She was flying the British flag. Scaife and I went down to the port and spoke to the coastguard there. We said that we wanted to go fishing. So the coastguard got a boat for us, and we sailed out of the port.

We caught a lot of fish that afternoon. And at about four o'clock we sailed quite close to the sailing boat. She looked like a beautiful white bird on the water.

'She's a fast boat,' Scaife said. 'If anyone wants to get away quickly, they'll go in a ship like this.'

Her name was the *Ariadne*. We spoke to a few men on her, and they were clearly Englishmen. Then an officer joined them, and the men stopped talking. The officer was a young man and he spoke English very well. But we were quite sure that he was not an Englishman. His hair was cut very short and his clothes looked quite foreign.

In the evening I met the captain of the warship at the hotel.

'We'll probably need your ship tonight or tomorrow,' I said. 'Has anyone spoken to you about that?'

'Yes, sir. I've had a message from the Admiralty. I'll come in close when it's dark. I know what to do.'

About an hour later I walked back along the hill-top towards Trafalgar Lodge. The old man and a young man were playing tennis in the garden. While I was watching them, a woman brought out bottles and glasses. The young man, who was rather fat, took the things from her.

'Those people seem all right,' I said to myself. 'They're quite different from those terrible men in Scotland. I've probably made a mistake.'

Then another man arrived at the house on a bicycle. He was thin, dark and quite young. They finished the game of tennis and they all went into the house.

I walked slowly back to the hotel. Was I wrong about those men? Were they acting while I was watching them? They did not know that anyone was watching them. And they were acting like any other Englishmen.

But there *were* three men in that house: the old man, the fat one and the thin, dark man. The house fitted Scudder's description. A sailing boat was lying less than a kilometre away and she had a foreign officer. I thought about Karolides and the danger of war. And I remembered the fear in Sir Arthur Drew's face.

I knew what I had to do. I had to go to that house and arrest those men. If I was wrong, it was my problem. But I did not like the job at all.

Suddenly I remembered my friend Peter Pienaar in Rhodesia. Peter was a criminal before he became a policeman. In fact the police accepted him for that reason. He knew all the worst criminals in the country. Peter told me that he once got away from the police very easily. He put on a black coat and went to church. And he chose to sit next to a police officer. They sang together and used the same book. And the policeman did not know who Peter was! I asked him why. And Peter replied, 'Because the place and my clothes were different. He knew me in my usual clothes, in a street or at a hotel. But he could not imagine me in church or wearing a long black coat.'

These thoughts made me feel more comfortable. Our German enemies were as clever as Peter. They lived in an English house, and the British flag was flying in the garden. They used English names and played English games. Their private life was completely English, and so nobody thought twice about them.

It was now eight o'clock in the evening. I met Scaife at the hotel and gave him his orders.

'Put two men in the garden,' I said, 'and hide three others close to the windows. When I want you, I'll call.'

I was not hungry, so I went for a walk. I saw the lights on the *Ariadne* and on the warship. I sat down on a seat and waited for more than an hour.

At half past nine I went to Trafalgar Lodge. Scaife's men were in their places by now, but I did not see anyone. There were lights in the house and the windows were open. I pushed the doorbell. One of the women opened the door.

'May I speak to Mr Appleton?' I asked.

'Yes, sir. Please come in,' she said.

I had a plan. I hoped to walk straight into the house and to watch those three German faces. But when I was inside, I felt less sure of myself. I saw their hats and coats and walking sticks in the hall. There was a large clock in one corner. English pictures were hanging on the walls, and the place was like thousands of other English homes.

'Your name, sir?' the woman asked.

'Hannay. Richard Hannay.'

She went into a room and called my name. I followed just behind her, but I was too late. The three men had a moment to hide their surprise.

The old man was standing up, and he and the fat one were wearing dinner-suits. The other man was in a suit of blue cloth.

'Mr Hannay?' the old man said. 'You want to speak to me, I believe. Come into the next room, please.'

I pulled a chair towards me and sat down on it.

'You know me,' I said, 'and you know my business.'

The light was not very good in the room. But I saw that they all looked surprised.

'Perhaps we do know you,' the old man said, 'but I can't remember. I'm sorry that I don't know your business, sir. Will you please tell me?'

I thought about Peter Pienaar and said, 'This is the end. I've come to arrest you all.'

'Arrest us!' the old man said. 'But why?'

'I'm arresting you for the murder of Franklin Scudder in London on 23 May.'

'I don't know that name,' the old man said, and his voice seemed very weak.

The fat man spoke then. 'I read about that in the papers. But this is terrible. We don't know anything about the murder, sir. Where do you come from?'

'Scotland Yard,' I said.

There was a silence when they heard that. The old man looked down at his feet and seemed very nervous.

Then the fat man said, 'This is surely a mistake, uncle. We can easily prove our stories. I wasn't even in England on 23 May, and you were ill, weren't you, Bob? You were in London, uncle, I know; but you can explain your business there.'

'That's right, Percy! Now what did I do on 23 May? Oh, I remember. I came up in the morning from Woking and had dinner with Charlie Symons. I was at Grantham House in the afternoon, wasn't I? Yes, that's right. And I stayed there all evening.'

The fat man looked at me. 'I'm afraid you've made a mistake, sir. We'll help you if we can, of course. But sometimes Scotland Yard is wrong.'

'Yes, of course,' the old man said. 'We'll do anything to help you, sir, but this is clearly a mistake.'

'Won't Nellie laugh when she hears about this!' one of them said.

'Oh, she will! I can't wait to tell Charlie about it too. Now, Mr Hannay, I'm not angry with you, but you've come to the wrong place.'

Surely they weren't acting. What they said was all true. It *was* my mistake. And I wanted to say, 'I'm sorry,' and leave the house.

But the old man had very little hair. The fat man was there too, and the third man was dark and thin. I looked at them and I looked around the room. Everything was all right and in its place. And I did not know their faces.

'Don't you agree, sir?' the old man asked me. 'Haven't you come to the wrong house?'

'No. This is the right house.'

'Well, we have other things to do with our time,' the thin man said. 'Are you going to take us to the police station? You're only doing your job, I know, but it's very difficult.'

I did not answer him. I thought, 'Oh, Peter Pienaar, help me!'

The fat man stood up. 'Perhaps Mr Hannay needs more time,'

he said. 'It isn't an easy problem for him. Let's play cards for half an hour, shall we? Do you play, sir?'

'Yes. I've got a lot of time and I like a game of cards.' We went into the next room, and I looked around. Books and newspapers were lying around. The tennis things were in an open cupboard in the corner.

We sat around a card-table in the middle of the room. And the dark man brought me a drink. I played with him against the others.

It was like a dream. The windows were open, and I could see the moonlight on the sea. The three men were not afraid at all. They were talking and laughing together. But my heart was beating very quickly.

I did not play very well that night. My thoughts were too ugly for me to follow the cards. I was not sure about these men, and they knew it of course. I looked at their faces again and again but did not know them. They did not only seem different. I felt sure that they *were* different. 'Oh, Peter,' I thought once more.

Then suddenly I saw something. The old man put down his cards to drink some wine. And he did not pick them up for a moment. He sat back in his chair and began to play with his right ear. I remembered that Scottish farm. I was standing in front of him again after telling him my story. And, there, in Scotland, he sat back and played with his ear. It was only a little thing, but I remembered it well.

The clouds lifted from my eyes and everything was clear again. The faces of the three men changed suddenly and I knew all their secrets. It was the dark man who killed Scudder. I was playing cards with him, but his eyes looked cold and hard now. The fat man was different too. He did not have one face but a hundred faces. And he was probably the Lord Alloa of the night before. But the old man was clearly the chief criminal. He was as hard as rock and quite without fear. I remembered Scudder's

*We sat around a card-table in the middle of the room.*

words: 'If you see his eyes, Hannay, you'll never forget them.' And it was true.

We continued to play, but my heart was full of hate. When the dark man spoke to me, I could not answer him.

'Bob! Look at the clock,' the old man said. 'You'll miss your train if we don't hurry.' He turned to me. 'Bob has to go back to London tonight.' The voice was now as completely false as their faces.

'I'm sorry,' I said, 'but he isn't going tonight.'

'Why not?' the young man asked. 'I *have* to go. I'll give you my address.'

'No. You have to stay here.'

That probably made them nervous. They knew that I knew them. They had only one chance now, and the old man took it.

'Well, arrest me, Mr Hannay, and let the others go. Will that be all right?'

I shouted, 'Scaife!'

The lights went out. Strong arms held me, and I could not move.

'*Schnell, Franz,*' a voice cried, '*zum Boot, zum Boot!*'

I looked out of the window. Two police officers were running across the garden. The dark man jumped through the window and was running towards the steps. Suddenly the room filled with people, and I was free. I caught the old man and held him. Scaife and another policeman fell on the fat one. The lights came on.

We looked out of the window again. Franz reached the steps before the policemen. He opened the gate, which locked itself behind him. And the policemen could not follow. We waited for a few minutes.

Suddenly the old man was free again. He hurried to the wall of the room and pushed something. A great noise rose up from below the house. The steps flew into the air.

'Dynamite!' I cried. 'They've destroyed the stairs!'

*A great noise rose up from below the house. The steps flew into the air.*

The old man was looking at me and laughing. A terrible light burned in his eyes.

'He is safe,' he shouted. 'You cannot follow him. He has gone . . . He has won. *Der schwarze Stein ist in der Siegesthrone!*'

Two police officers caught the old man by the arms, and I said my last words to him.

'Franz hasn't won anything. He'll reach the *Ariadne* quite safely, I'm sure. But she was in our hands an hour ago.'

Everyone knows that the war began early in August 1914. That was about six weeks after I helped to catch those three German spies. I was an officer during those unhappy war years. But perhaps my best work was done before it started.

# ACTIVITIES

## Chapters 1–2
*Before you read*
1 What do you know about the First World War? Find out:
   a when it started.
   b who started it.
   c which countries fought in it.
   d the reasons for the war.
2 Find these words in your dictionary. Use them in the sentences below.
   politics   Prime Minister
   a The.................... is the head of the government in the UK.
   b If you want to work in government, you should study .................

*After you read*
3 Are these sentences true or false?
   a Hannay knows Scudder very well.
   b Scudder's enemies are foreign spies.
   c Hannay is very interested in politics.
   d Hannay reports Scudder's death to the police.
   e He is afraid of Scudder's enemies.
   f He decides to hide in Scotland.
4 Why does Hannay decide to continue Scudder's work?
5 Work in pairs and use your imagination.
   Student A: You are Scudder. You are very frightened. Ask your neighbour for help.
   Student B: You are yourself and you live in the same building as Scudder. Open the door to him and ask about his problems. Then decide what you are going to do.

## Chapters 3–4
*Before you read*
6 What do you think that:
   a Hannay will do in Scotland?
   b the milkman will do in London?
   c Scudder's enemies will do?

**7** Find these words in your dictionary. Match the words with their meanings.

*arrest   code   Sir   telegram*

| | |
|---|---|
| code | **a** a title that a man is given for success in life |
| arrest | **b** a message sent by radio |
| Sir | **c** numbers or letters that say something secretly |
| telegram | **d** to catch someone because they have done something wrong |

*After you read*

**8** Who says:
  **a** 'You have to change here.'
  **b** 'Please come in.'
  **c** 'Help! Help!'
  **d** 'I don't meet many interesting people.'
  **e** 'Stop! Stop!'
  **f** 'Are you hurt?'

**9** Two groups of people are looking for Hannay. Who are they?

**10** Work in pairs.
  *Student A:* You are the milkman. Explain what you were doing in Hannay's flat.
  *Student B:* You are a police officer. Ask the milkman questions. Do you believe his story?

**11** Imagine that you are Sir Harry. Describe your meeting with Richard Hannay. Then talk about the time that you spent with him.

## Chapters 5–6

*Before you read*

**12** Why is 15 June an important day?

**13** What does Hannay plan to do between now and 15 June?

**14** Find these words in your dictionary and use them in the sentence below.

*detonator   dynamite*

The soldiers used a [1]............... and some [2].................. to destroy the building.

*After you read:*

15  Complete the story. Write a word or phrase in each gap.
People are searching for Hannay on foot and ¹............... , so he borrows the clothes and job of a roadman. After a visit by the roadman's boss, Hannay is visited by ²............... . They are satisfied that Hannay is ³............... . The next car belongs to a man called ⁴............... . Hannay uses his car to ⁵............... . Then he runs to a farm to get away from ⁶............... . But the people in the farm are ⁷............... . They put him in ⁸............... . He uses dynamite from the cupboard to ⁹............... . From his new hiding place on the birdhouse, he can see ¹⁰............... .

16  Describe Hannay's worst enemy.

17  Hannay says: 'I decided that I was a very lucky man.' Do you agree? Explain why/why not.

## Chapters 7–8

*Before you read*

18  What do you think?
   a  How is Hannay feeling now?
   b  What does he look like?
   c  How is he going to get away from his enemies?

19  Find these words in your dictionary.
*Admiralty  butler  cottage  General  Lord*
Which word means:
   a  a small house?
   b  an important soldier?
   c  a government office?
   d  somebody who works in a big house?
   e  an important man?

*After you read:*

20  Give reasons for these people's actions and ideas.
   1  The woman at the cottage does not want any money from Hannay.
   a  The roadman does not want any money from Hannay.
   b  Hannay and the fisherman sing the song "Annie Laurie".

    **c** Sir Walter believes Hannay's story.
    **d** The police do not want to arrest him.
    **e** Sir Walter starts to believe Scudder's story.
    **f** Hannay decides to continue the fight.
    **g** He pushes a policeman to the ground.
    **h** Hannay telephones Lord Alloa's number.
**21** Work in pairs. Act out the first long conversation between Hannay and Sir Walter in your own words. You are in the library after dinner and Sir Walter wants to know everything.

## Chapters 9–10
*Before you read*
**22** Now the Black Stone group has the war plans. What will these people do next?
    **a** the Black Stone spies
    **b** Hannay and the other men in Sir Walter's meeting room

*After you read*
**23** Find these words in your dictionary. Are the sentences below true?
*captain   coastguard   tide*
    **a** The captain gives the orders on a ship.
    **b** A coastguard also works on a ship.
    **c** At high tide the sea covers more of the beach than at low tide.
**24** Why are these important to the story?
    **1** a lion
    **2** thirty-nine steps
    **3** the *Ariadne*
    **4** a man's right ear
**25** Imagine that you are the British Prime Minister. Make a speech. Thank Richard Hannay for his help in catching the Black Stone spies.

## Writing

26  When he is on a train, Hannay reads about the milkman in a newspaper. Write the newspaper story. Start like this: MURDER IN A LONDON FLAT.

27  Write a letter from Hannay to the roadman. Thank him for his help. Tell him your real reason for doing his job.

28  Choose two of these people and compare their jobs:
Scudder    the milkman    the innkeeper    the roadman
Sir Walter

29  Do you know a story about a successful spy? Why was that spy successful? Why were the Black Stone spies unsuccessful?

30  Would you like to read another book about Richard Hannay's adventures? Why/why not?

31  Did you learn anything surprising about Britain and British people 80 years ago? In what ways was life in Britain then different from life in your country now?

---

For a complete list of the titles available in the Penguin Readers series please write to your local Pearson Education office or to: Marketing Department, Penguin Longman Publishing, 5 Bentinck Street, London W1M 5RN.

# The Turn of the Screw

## HENRY JAMES

Level 3

Retold by Cherry Gilchrist
Series Editors: Andy Hopkins and Jocelyn Potter

## Contents

| | | page |
|---|---|---|
| Introduction | | 140 |
| Chapter 1 | A Governess Gets a Job | 143 |
| Chapter 2 | The Two Children | 146 |
| Chapter 3 | A Frightening Face | 151 |
| Chapter 4 | Two People Who Died | 155 |
| Chapter 5 | The Children in Danger | 158 |
| Chapter 6 | A Letter to Miles's Uncle | 163 |
| Chapter 7 | Flora Disappears | 170 |
| Chapter 8 | Trying to Save Miles | 173 |
| Activities | | 182 |

## Introduction

*'They were a wicked pair,' Mrs Grose said, 'but what can they do now? They're dead.'*
*'They're still here . . . They can still take Miles and Flora from us!'*

A young lady has come to a big country house to teach two young children. It is her first job and she is alone with the housekeeper, Mrs Grose. Strange things begin to happen. She sees a man on the roof of the house, and a woman by the lake, dressed in black. The man and woman are dead, so these are their ghosts. What do they want? Who are they looking for? And why?

A terrible story of fear and danger begins. The children are beautiful but are they good? Can the new governess help the children? Or will the ghosts of Peter Quint and Miss Jessel take Miles and Flora away?

Henry James wrote this famous story in 1898. He wrote it for an American magazine named *Collier's*. Later he put it into a book. It is one of the most famous ghost stories written in English. Benjamin Britten used the story to make a musical play with the same title.

Henry James was an American, born in New York in 1843. His father was a well-known writer and speaker, and his brother, William James, was a famous university teacher. As a young man, Henry James travelled widely in Europe and he also studied law at Harvard University. He began to write short stories in 1865. He moved to England in 1876 and stayed there for the rest of his life. He lived in the small town of Rye on the south coast. Many famous writers came to visit him there: Joseph Conrad, Ford Madox Ford and H. G. Wells. Wells became one of his greatest friends. Henry James wrote many famous books, among them

*Washington Square* (1880), *The Portrait of a Lady* (1881), *The Bostonians* (1886), *What Maisie Knew* (1887), *The Wings of the Dove* (1902), *The Ambassadors* (1903) and *The Golden Bowl* (1904). A number of these books have now become films. In 1915, James decided to become British and the King of England gave him the Order of Merit (a title which the king or queen gives to successful people in different areas of work). James died the following year.

Henry James writes about how people think and feel when they are unhappy or in love or afraid, or when they want to be rich or famous. The people in his books are usually people with plenty of money. They like to travel around the world. One of his favourite subjects is young Americans who visit Europe and make friends with Europeans. The Americans are usually rich and innocent and the Europeans are often clever and selfish: they want to get their hands on the Americans' money. Not many of James's stories have happy endings. By the end, the innocent people have usually become wiser: they don't believe everything that others tell them. Most of his stories take place in the real world. *The Turn of the Screw* is unusual because it is about ghosts.

The title of the book is rather strange. It means 'making the reader's feelings tighter', that is, stronger. In this story we feel fear and danger. We are afraid of what is going to happen to the two children. But we don't understand clearly what things the children have done. Are they really innocent? Did Quint and Miss Jessel teach them to be bad? If they really *are* bad, what bad things did they do? Why do the ghosts want to take them away? Will the children die?

Even when we get to the end of the story, we are still not able to answer most of these questions. Perhaps this is why the story seems so modern. All these unknown facts form a mystery which we go on thinking about. *The Turn of the Screw* is a story that is very difficult to forget.

## Chapter 1  A Governess Gets a Job

It was a strange story which we heard in that old house, on the night before Christmas. We sat by the fire and listened silently until the end. Then somebody said, 'How unusual! It's the first time that I've ever heard about a child who saw a ghost.'

I could see that Douglas wanted to say something. After a few seconds, he spoke. 'It's not the only time that a child has seen a ghost. A ghost story with one child in it is frightening enough. But two children who see ghosts – isn't that quite strange? Doesn't that give the story another turn of the screw?'

'Of course!' somebody answered. 'Two children give two turns of the screw! We want to hear the story!'

Douglas looked at all of us, and said quietly, 'It's a terrible story. It is the most frightening story that I know.'

'Then begin at once!' I said.

'I can't. It's in a book which is locked in my desk at home. I can ask my servant to put it in the post.'

'Oh yes! Please do!' Everyone asked him to hurry.

'Is it your story?' I asked him.

'No, no! I heard it from a woman. I've never forgotten it. She wrote it down, and when she died it came to me. She was ten years older than me. She was my sister's governess when I was a student at university. In the summer holidays I talked to her a lot. Yes – don't smile – she was beautiful. She was also clever and interesting, and I liked her very much. I think she liked me too. It was forty years ago, but I remember everything.'

'Did she tell any others her story?'

'No, she said that I was the first person to hear it.'

The packet arrived in the post two days later. We all wanted to hear the story, and we sat down ready after dinner that evening.

Before Douglas read the story to us, he told us about the young woman. She was twenty years old; she came from a poor, church family, and she decided to work as a governess. She heard about a man who wanted to employ a governess for two children. She went to London and met him at his large house in Harley Street. They were his brother's children; his brother was dead, and now he had to look after them.

The man was handsome, rich, and unmarried, and the young woman was immediately in love with him.

'I'll be so pleased if you can take the job!' he told her. 'London isn't a good place for children. I've taken them to my family home in Essex* – it's a large house with big gardens and a park. I have no time to look after them. I've sent my best servants there, and the housekeeper, Mrs Grose, is a very good woman. You will like her, I'm sure.'

He was very worried about the children, a little girl and her older brother. Not long ago, their first governess died suddenly, and now their uncle had to employ a new governess quickly. He had to find the right person. The boy was away at school, but he came back in the holidays, and the little girl was home all the time.

'How did the first governess die?' a listener asked Douglas. 'Was the job dangerous?'

'You will hear everything,' he answered.

The young lady did not give her answer at once. It was her first job; and the house was big, and almost empty. The money was good, but could she be happy there, alone? She wanted to help this wonderful man, but could she look after the children well enough?

She returned to the house in Harley Street two days later.

'I have decided to take the job,' she said.

---

* Essex: a part of England in the east of the country.

'I'll be so pleased if you can take the job!' he told her.

'Her love for her new master —' somebody said.

'Yes, of course. This love helped her later — it helped her to be brave,' Douglas continued. 'But her employer said, "There's one thing that you must promise me. You must never bring any problem to me. You must never write to me. You must decide everything."'

She promised. He took her hand; he was so pleased with her. She never saw him again.

Douglas opened the red book on his knee, and began to read the governess's story to us.

## Chapter 2  The Two Children

I was very worried during the journey. Was I making a mistake? I was going alone to a strange house, to teach two children that I did not know. But it was a beautiful day, and when I arrived, the house was a pleasant surprise. It was large, but light, with open windows and bright flowers in the gardens. And Flora was the most beautiful child that I have ever seen. Her hair was gold in colour, and her dress was blue. She and Mrs Grose, the housekeeper, were there to meet me.

Mrs Grose seemed to be a kind, good woman, and at supper that evening, I asked her about Miles, the boy.

'If you like this little girl, you will like the boy, too,' she said. She smiled at Flora, and Flora smiled at us both. 'He's so clever.'

'When will I see him? Tomorrow?'

'No, the day after.'

I was very excited that night, and did not sleep much. I heard some small sounds in the house; perhaps someone was awake. My room was large and comfortable. There was a little bed in it for Flora, but on my first night she slept with Mrs Grose. I woke up with the birds, and looked forward to my first full day with her.

*When I arrived, the house was a pleasant surprise.*

Flora showed me everything in the house and garden. She showed me the secret places, the old stairs, the empty rooms. After half an hour we were good friends.

'Perhaps,' I thought, 'I'm in some wonderful story. But, no, it's real, and it will be an adventure for me.'

I remembered my promise to my employer that evening. A letter came from Miles's school. I was not excited now, but worried. The head at the school wrote that Miles could not go back there again.

'They won't take him back!' I told Mrs Grose.

'Never?' she asked, surprised.

'Never. Here, you can read the letter.'

I gave it to her but she shook her head sadly.

'I cannot read,' she said. 'What has he done?' she was almost crying.

'They don't say. But they think that he's dangerous to the other children.'

'Dangerous?' Mrs Grose was angry now.

'Is he a bad child?'

'He's only ten years old! How can he be bad? Is she bad?' She pointed at Flora, who was sitting quietly at the table. The little girl was writing, practising her letter 'O's.

'Naughty, then?' I asked her.

'Oh yes, of course, he is sometimes naughty! But–'

'Every boy must be naughty sometimes.'

'Yes! A boy who is not naughty is not a boy for me!'

Later, before Miles arrived, I asked her about the last governess.

'What kind of lady was she?'

'She was young and pretty like you.'

'Was she careful with the boy?'

'With some things – yes. But perhaps not with everything. But she's dead now, so I mustn't speak badly of her.'

'Yes, of course,' I said, quickly. 'Was she ill? Did she die here?'

*The head at the school wrote that Miles could not go back there again. 'They won't take him back!' I told Mrs Grose.*

*'He can't be bad! It's not possible! Look at him!'*

'No, she went for a holiday. Then she died – the master told me.'
'How did she die?'
'He didn't say.' And she would not tell me any more.

Miles was as beautiful as his sister. I loved him too, as soon as I saw him. He had a sweet innocence, and I could not understand the school's letter.

'He can't be bad! It's not possible!' I said to Mrs Grose later. 'Look at him!'

'Yes, I look at him all the time,' she smiled. 'What will you do?'

'I won't answer the letter. I can't write to his uncle. And I won't speak to Miles about it.'

'Good!' Mrs Grose said. 'Then together we'll be friends to the two children.' She kissed me like a sister.

## Chapter 3   A Frightening Face

I did not give the children many lessons during those first weeks. Perhaps *they* were teaching *me* now – they were teaching me to laugh, to play, to be free. I was more innocent than the children. I know that now.

In the evenings, when they were in bed, I liked to walk among the summer flowers in the gardens, and under the old trees in the park. Sometimes I could see the face of my employer in front of my eyes. 'He's smiling at me,' I thought. 'He's pleased with me – I'm looking after the children well for him.'

One evening in June, I walked about three miles through the park. When I came back to the house, I looked up and saw a face. Was it my employer's face which I thought about so much? No, it was not – I realised that very quickly. A man stood on the roof of the tower. There were two towers, one at each end of the roof. Each tower had a room inside, and you could climb out onto the roof from them; Flora took me there on my first day. I did not know this man. I saw him very clearly, and he was watching me. He stood still and stared at me for a minute, then turned away.

I was frightened. Was there a secret in this old house? I wanted to ask Mrs Grose, but when I came back into the house, everything seemed quite ordinary again. I did not say anything to her, but for many days I thought about it. Finally I decided, 'It was a stranger who found a way into the house. But he's gone now, so I can forget him. I won't worry about it.'

I preferred to enjoy my days with the children. I was never bored with them. They were happy, and they made me happy too. I did not think about my family at home now; Flora and Miles were my family, and this was my home.

One Sunday, in the early evening, Mrs Grose and I decided to go to church together. My bag was in the dining-room, and I went in there to get it. Suddenly, I looked up and saw a face at the window. It was staring at me through the glass. It was the man who I saw on the roof. I stared at him; he stared at me. I did not know him, but I felt, strangely, that I knew him very well. Then he looked round the room.

'He's looking for someone, but not for me!' I realised.

Then I felt brave. I ran outside and looked for him. But he was not there. The garden was empty. I went back to the window, put my face against the glass, and stared in. Mrs Grose walked into the dining-room, and saw me. She turned white, and came outside to meet me.

'Why is *she* frightened?' I asked myself.

'What's the matter?' she asked me. 'Your face is white. You look terrible.'

'*My* face?' I said. 'I was frightened. You saw my face at the window, but when I was in the dining-room, I saw a man's face in the same place.'

'Who is he? Where has he gone?'

*Suddenly, I looked up and saw a face at the window. It was staring at me through the glass.*

'I have no idea.'

'Have you seen him before?'

'Yes – once. He was standing on the roof of the tower.'

'And you didn't tell me? What was he doing there?'

'He looked at me – that's all. He was a stranger, a dreadful man.'

Mrs Grose looked out over the gardens once more, then said, 'Well, it's time for church now.'

'No, I can't go to church. Not now. I can't leave the children. It's not safe.'

'It isn't safe?' she asked.

'He's dangerous!' I replied.

She realised something then. I could see it in her face.

'What did he look like?' she asked.

'He is like nobody!'

'What do you mean?'

'He has no hat!' She looked worried, so I continued quickly, 'He has red hair, and a long face, with strange eyes.'

Mrs Grose's mouth was open, and she stared at me. Is he handsome? How is he dressed?'

'Oh, yes, he's handsome. And he's wearing another person's clothes.'

'The master's!' she said.

'You know this man?'

She did not reply for a second, then she answered, 'Quint. Peter Quint. He was the master's servant. He took some of his clothes – but never his hat. When the master left, Quint looked after everything in the house. He was only a servant, but he gave the orders.'

'Then where did he go?'

'Go?' she said. 'Oh no, he died.'

'Died?' I almost screamed.

'Yes,' she said. 'Peter Quint is dead.'

## Chapter 4  Two People Who Died

Mrs Grose and I talked a lot about Quint's ghost.

'I have never seen anything,' she said. But she knew my story was true. 'Who was he looking for?' she asked me.

'He was looking for little Miles,' I said, because suddenly I knew that it was true.

Mrs Grose looked frightened. 'The child?' she asked.

'His ghost wants to find the children.'

'How do you know?'

'I know, I know! And you know too, don't you?' She did not answer, so I continued, 'Miles never speaks about Quint. Isn't that strange? He says nothing to me. "They were great friends, Miles and Quint," you told me.'

'It was Quint's idea,' Mrs Grose said. 'He wanted to play with Miles all the time. He was too free with him.'

'Too free!' He was too free with my boy! – this was terrible.

'He was too free with everyone.'

'So he was truly a bad man?'

'I knew it, but the master didn't. He didn't like to hear about any sort of trouble. I couldn't tell him. I was afraid.'

'What were you afraid of?'

'Quint was so clever – he could do terrible things.'

'A dreadful man, with those innocent little children – couldn't you do something?'

'I couldn't say anything. Peter Quint gave the orders.' She began to cry.

Did Mrs Grose tell me everything? No – there was something that she didn't say. I had to be brave. I had to watch carefully. The children must not meet this ghost!

And then, one afternoon, I took Flora out into the garden. Miles was reading inside, so Flora and I walked down to the lake together. It was hot, and we walked under the trees for much of the time. When we arrived at the lake, I sat down with a book, and for an hour everything was quiet. Suddenly I thought, 'Someone is watching us.' But I did not look up at once. I looked at Flora first. She had stopped playing and was very still. 'She can see the person too!' I thought. Then she turned away quickly from the lake.

Now I had to look up. A woman was standing on the other side of the lake — a dreadful woman, dressed in black. She was staring at Flora. I knew that she was the ghost of Miss Jessel, the children's old governess.

'Flora saw her too!' I told Mrs Grose later.

'Did she tell you?' Mrs Grose asked.

'No — and that makes it more terrible! The woman has come for Flora. The way she looks at her —'

Mrs Grose turned white. 'She was dressed in black?'

'Yes, and she was handsome. She was a beautiful woman, but a bad one.'

'They were both bad,' she said at last.

'You must tell me about them now,' I said.

'They were — together,' she said. 'They were lovers. But she paid a terrible price for it. Yes, she suffered, poor woman! He did what he wanted.'

'With her?'

'With them all.'

'How did she die?'

'I don't know. I didn't want to know. But she couldn't stay in the house after that. She had to leave. She was a lady, and he was only a servant.'

'And Peter Quint? How did he die?'

'He drank too much one night. He came out of the bar in the village and fell down on the ice. He cut his head on a stone. Well, that's what people say. Nobody really knows.'

'It's all so terrible!' And now I began to cry, and Mrs Grose took me in her arms. 'We can't save the children! They're lost! Lost!'

*A woman was standing on the other side of the lake – a dreadful woman, dressed in black.*

But I still wanted to be with the children most of all, specially with Flora. She looked into my face carefully with her big, blue eyes, and said, 'You were crying.' She was so sweet, so innocent – how could she know about these dreadful things?

And Miles? I asked Mrs Grose about Miles. '"He was sometimes bad," you said to me. How was he bad?'

'Naughty,' she replied. 'I said naughty, not bad.'

'Please tell me!' I continued. 'He's always so good with me. So when he was bad – or naughty – it was unusual. What happened?'

We were talking late into the night, and now the grey light of morning was coming. Mrs Grose was silent for a minute, then she answered me.

'Quint and the boy were together all the time. I didn't like it. I spoke to Miss Jessel about it. She was angry with me. "It's none of your business," she said. So I spoke to Miles.'

'You told him that Peter Quint was only a servant?'

'Yes. "You're only a servant too," he answered me. And there were times when he and Peter Quint were together for hours, but he said, "I haven't seen Peter today."'

'He lied to you?'

Mrs Grose seemed surprised by this word. 'Yes – perhaps he did.'

'And he knew about Quint, and Miss Jessel?'

'I don't know – I don't know!'

'Yes, you *do* know! And we need to know more!'

## Chapter 5   The Children in Danger

I waited and watched carefully for some days. The children were so lovable and happy that I nearly forgot my worries sometimes. They enjoyed studying, and were clever and funny in our lessons together. Sometimes they seemed to have a plan: one of them talked to me, while the other disappeared outside. But this did not really worry me.

Then, one evening, I stayed up very late in my bedroom. I was reading a book by the light of a candle. Flora was asleep in her little bed in the corner. Suddenly, I looked up and listened. Something was moving in the house. I remembered my first night, when I heard sounds like this.

I took my candle and left the room. I locked the door behind me, and walked to the top of the stairs. My candle went out, but I noticed that it was already quite light, and I could see without it. I realised that there was someone on the stairs below. It was Peter Quint again. There was a big window by the stairs, he stood by it and stared up at me. I knew then that he was both wicked and dangerous. But I was not afraid. We stood and stared silently, and that was the strangest thing. A murderer can talk, but a ghost cannot. Then he turned, and disappeared at the bottom of the stairs.

I returned to my room. A candle was still burning there, and I saw that Flora's bed was empty. I ran to her bed, frightened. Then I heard a sound. She was hiding by the window. She looked very serious.

'You naughty person! Where did you go?'

I sat down, and she climbed onto my knee.

'Were you looking for me out of the window?' I asked her. 'Did you think I was in the garden?'

'Well, someone was out there,' she said, and smiled at me. Her face was innocent and beautiful in the candlelight.

'And did you see anybody?'

'Oh, no!'

I knew that she was lying. But I did not say anything.

Each night now I sat up late. Sometimes I went out of my room to look, and listen. Once I saw a woman on the stairs. She sat there in sadness, with her head in her hands. She did not show me her face, but I knew that it was dreadful and that she was

*Flora was standing by the window ... There was a full moon, and I could see her face in its light.*

suffering. I only saw her for a second, and then she disappeared.

After eleven nights, I could not stay awake late, and I went to sleep quite early. I woke up at about one o'clock in the morning. Flora was standing by the window, staring out. She did not notice me. There was a full moon, and I could see her face in its light. She was giving herself to something out there, to the ghost that we saw by the lake. I got up – I wanted to find another room with windows that looked out onto the garden.

The room in the tower was the best one. It was a big, cold bedroom, nobody ever slept there. I put my face against the glass of the window. The garden was very bright in the moonlight. Somebody was standing on the grass and staring up above me – at the tower. So there was another person out there, on the roof of the tower. But the person in the garden was not the ghost of the woman. It was little Miles.

When I went down into the garden, Miles came in quietly with me, back to his bedroom.

'Tell me now, Miles,' I said. 'Why did you go out? What were you doing in the garden?'

'Will you understand?' he asked me, with his wonderful smile. I felt almost sick while I waited to hear. He planned to tell me everything!

'Well,' he said. 'I wanted to be bad!' He kissed me. 'I didn't go to bed! I went out at midnight! When I'm bad, I'm really bad!' He spoke like a naughty, happy child. 'I planned it with Flora.'

'She stood at the window–'

'To wake you up!'

'And you stood outside in the cold. Well, you must go to bed now.' I was the governess again, and Miles was just a naughty boy. He was too clever for me.

I told Mrs Grose everything. 'We think that the children are good, but they're not. They live with *them* – not with us. They want to be with Quint and that woman!'

'They're still here! Their ghosts are looking for our children.'

'But why?' Mrs Grose asked.

'Because Peter Quint and Miss Jessel are wicked, and they taught Flora and Miles to love wickedness. They're bad!'

'Yes, they were a wicked pair,' Mrs Grose said. 'But what can they do now? They're dead.'

'They're still here! Their ghosts are looking for our children. They can still take Miles and Flora from us!'

'Oh, my goodness!'

'They wait in high, strange or dangerous places – the roof of the tower, the other side of the lake. It's dangerous but exciting, for Flora and Miles. They'll try to get to those wicked people.'

'And a terrible accident can happen – I see,' said Mrs Grose. 'We must stop this. Their uncle must take them away from here. I can't write, so you must write to him.'

'What can I say? How will he know that it's true?' ('My employer will be angry with me,' I thought. 'I wanted so much to be brave and to help him.')

Mrs Grose took my arm. 'He must come!' she said. 'He must come back and help us!'

## Chapter 6  A Letter to Miles's Uncle

The summer changed into the autumn. I didn't see any more ghosts, and I did nothing. The sky was grey, and dead leaves blew onto the grass. Did the children see things? Sometimes everything suddenly went quiet in the schoolroom. I think that wicked pair were with us then. I think, too, that the children could see them. But usually, they were happy and worked hard. They were very interested in their uncle.

'Will he come soon?' they asked me. They wrote beautiful letters to him.

'We can't send them to him,' I explained. 'He's too busy. Perhaps he'll come later in the year.'

I wanted to speak to the children about the ghosts, but I couldn't find a way. They stayed silent about them, and so did I. Sometimes, alone, I thought about it all night, but my thoughts stayed secret. Everything felt heavy, like a storm was coming.

Then the storm came. I was walking to church one Sunday morning with Miles. Flora and Mrs Grose were in front. It was bright, cold autumn weather now.

'Can you tell me,' Miles said, 'when I'm going back to school?'

His voice was sweet, but the words surprised me. I stopped suddenly. He smiled at me. 'I'm a boy, you know. And I'm getting older now. I'm with a lady all the time – is it a good idea? She's a wonderful lady, of course – but a boy needs other boys and men.'

We walked on now. 'Were you happy at school?' I asked him.

He thought for a second. 'Oh, I'm happy enough anywhere.'

'Then you must be happy here too!'

'Yes, but I want – I want more interesting things to see and do.'

'I see,' I said.

'Does my uncle know about me, about everything?'

'I don't think he's interested, Miles,' I answered.

'Then he must come and visit us!'

'Who will ask him?'

'I will!' Miles said.

We were at the church now, but I did not go in. I stayed outside. For the first time, I did not want to be with Miles. Of course, he was right – it was unnatural for a boy to spend all his time with a governess, every day. And I was doing nothing about it. Could I speak to his uncle? Miles knew now that I did not want to do this.

'He'll use it in his plan!' I thought. He and Flora looked

'Can you tell me,' Miles said, 'when I'm going back to school?'

innocent, but they were not. 'I must leave this house! I'll go back and get ready. I can leave today!'

In the house, I went up to the school room for my books. I opened the door. But there, sitting at my table, was that dreadful woman – Miss Jessel. She was writing – I knew it – to her lover, Quint. Her tired face was full of suffering. She was using my pen, my paper. She stood up, and for a few seconds she looked at me. I stared at her, then I screamed, 'You're a wicked, terrible woman!' She seemed to hear me. But the next minute the room was empty. And I knew now that I must stay in the house. I could not leave.

'I've talked to Miss Jessel,' I said to Mrs Grose later, by the fire.

Mrs Grose was surprised, but she stayed calm. 'And what did she say?'

'She's suffering. She wants Flora. I've decided to write to the children's uncle.'

'Oh yes!' Mrs Grose said. 'You must.'

'I'll tell him this,' I said. ' "I cannot teach a boy who is wicked. The school have sent him home because of his wickedness." '

'But – we don't know –'

'Yes, we do,' I said. 'He *seems* to be so good, that he *must* be wicked, really wicked. I'll write tonight!'

I began the letter that evening. There was a strong wind and heavy rain outside. But it was quiet in my room, and Flora was asleep in her little bed. I stood up, took my candle and went to Miles's bedroom door. I listened. He called out, 'Come in! I can hear you outside!'

He was awake but in bed.

'Aren't you sleeping?' I asked him.

'No,' he answered, quite happily. 'I like to lie and think.'

'What do you think about?'

'About you, of course! And about all these strange things –'

'What strange things?'

*She stood up, and for a few seconds she looked at me. I stared at her, then I screamed.*

'Oh, you know!'

I held his hand, and he smiled up at me. 'Of course you can go back to school,' I said. 'But we must find a new one for you.' He looked so young, and innocent in his bed. 'You didn't say anything before,' I continued. 'What do you really want?'

He shook his head. 'I want to go away! Oh – you know what a boy wants!'

Do I? 'You want to go to your uncle?' I asked him.

'He must come here.'

'Yes, but he'll take you away, Miles.'

'That's what I want! You must tell him everything.'

'Tell him what?' I asked. 'He'll ask you questions. You must tell him things, too.'

'What things?'

'The things that you don't tell me. He must decide on his plans for you. You can't go back to your old school, you know.'

I looked at this brave, calm, young boy, and I kissed him with love.

'I'm writing to your uncle,' I said. 'I've already started the letter.'

'Well then, finish it!'

'Tell me something first, Miles. What happened?' He looked at me, surprised. 'What happened here in this house? What happened at school?' He was still looking at me. I held my arms out to him.

'Oh Miles!' I said. 'Dear little Miles, I want to help you! I don't want to hurt you. I want to help you so much!' But I knew at once that this was a mistake. Suddenly, there was a loud and terrible noise, a crash against the window. The cold wind blew into the room. Miles screamed.

I jumped up. Everything was dark.

'The candle has gone out!' I said.

'I blew it out, my dear,' Miles said.

*I looked at this brave, calm, young boy, and I kissed him with love.*

## Chapter 7  Flora Disappears

After the children's lessons the next day, Mrs Grose asked me, 'Have you written the letter?'

'Yes, I've written it.' I did not tell her that it was still in my pocket. I had to send it, I knew that now. Later, I put it on the table by the front door. 'One of the servants will find it, and take it to town,' I thought.

In the afternoon, Miles came to me. 'Shall I play some music for you?' he asked. He knew that he was winning, and that he was free now. He did not need to fight me, he could be friendly. The music was strange and beautiful. I was almost asleep. When it finished, I jumped up.

'Where's Flora?' I asked.

'How do I know?' Miles replied. He laughed, and started to play again.

I looked in my room, but Flora was not there. I went to Mrs Grose. Mrs Grose did not know where she was.

'Perhaps she's in one of the empty rooms,' she said. 'I thought that she was with you.'

Usually, I stayed with Flora all the time. 'No, she's outside, somewhere quite far away,' I answered. Mrs Grose looked surprised.

'Without a hat?' she asked.

'That woman that doesn't wear a hat!' I said. 'She's with *her*! We must find them!'

Mrs Grose did not move. 'And where is Miles?'

'Oh, *he's* with Quint in the schoolroom! He stayed with me so that Flora could get away! He's free now, he can do what he likes.'

We stood by the front door. The afternoon was grey, and the grass was wet.

'You aren't wearing your outdoor clothes!' Mrs Grose said.

'It doesn't matter! Flora hasn't got outdoor clothes on either,' I replied. 'I can't wait to dress! If you want to dress you must stay behind! Look for Flora upstairs!'

'And see *him*?' was her frightened reply. She came outside with me at once.

We walked quickly to the lake. I was sure that Flora was there.

'She wanted to go back there alone,' I explained to Mrs Grose. 'She and Miles planned this. And I'm sure that Miss Jessel is by the lake now.'

We arrived at the lake, but we could not see Flora.

'She's taken the boat,' I said, 'and hidden it on the other side. We must walk round and find her!'

'How could she do all that? She's only a little girl!'

'No, sometimes she's an old, old woman,' I said. 'And there's someone with her. You'll see.'

Ten minutes later, we arrived at the other side of the lake, and found the boat there. But where was Flora? We went on, into the next field.

'There she is!' we both said at the same time.

Flora stood on the grass and smiled. She did not move or speak. She smiled and smiled, in a dreadful, silent way. Mrs Grose threw her arms round the child.

Flora stared in surprise at my head, without its hat, and said, 'Where are your outdoor things?'

'Where are yours?' I asked her.

'And where's Miles?' she asked.

'If you'll tell me, I'll tell you –' There must be no secrets now.

'Tell you what?'

'Tell me, my dear – Where's Miss Jessel?'

Mrs Grose gave a small scream. In the same second, I screamed too – I shook Mrs Grose's arm and said, 'She's there, she's there!'

Miss Jessel stood on the other side of the lake. In a way, I was glad. 'It's all true, then,' I thought. 'Mrs Grose will be able to see everything, too.'

*I shook Mrs Grose's arm and said, 'She's there, she's there!'*

I pointed across the lake. Mrs Grose looked, but Flora did not. She watched my face calmly and seriously.

'She's there, you poor unhappy child! You can see her very well!'

But Mrs Grose was angry, 'What terrible things you say! Where can you see someone? There's nobody there!'

She could not see anything! And now I was losing everything! That wicked governess was winning!

'She's not there,' Mrs Grose continued, talking to Flora now. 'You can't see anyone! That poor lady – poor Miss Jessel's dead – we know that, don't we? It's all a mistake, and we're going home now, quickly.'

Flora was holding on to Mrs Grose's dress. Her face was suddenly ugly. 'I can't see anybody! I never see anything! I don't like you.' She turned towards Mrs Grose. 'Take me away from her!'

'From *me*?' I asked.

'From you – from you!'

I stared at the ghost, which was still there. Then I shook my head and said sadly to Flora, 'I've lost you. I'm sorry. She's won. I tried to help you. Goodbye.' And to Mrs Grose I said, 'Go! Go at once!'

I don't remember anything after that. I was on the ground, crying, for a very long time. It was nearly evening when I got up. I went back to the house and up to my room. Flora's things weren't there now. Later, Miles came and sat silently with me. He was not unfriendly. I was very cold, but felt warm when he was there.

## Chapter 8   Trying to Save Miles

Mrs Grose came into my room the next morning. Flora was ill.

'What does she say?' I asked. 'What has she seen?'

'I can't ask her,' Mrs Grose said sadly. 'But she seems so old now.'

'Does she talk about Miss Jessel?'

'Not a word.'

'They're so clever, that woman and Flora! Flora will never speak to me again. And she'll tell her uncle about me. "What a terrible governess!" he'll think. Shall I leave now?' I continued. 'That's what Flora wants, isn't it?'

She agreed. 'She doesn't want to see you again.'

'Well then,' I said, '*you* must go. You must take Flora away, to her uncle's. I'll stay here with Miles. But the two children must not meet alone together! Not for three seconds!'

'Yes, you're right. Flora must leave this house. We'll go this morning. And — I can't stay! Flora is saying such terrible things. Dreadful words, dreadful things. Where did she learn them?'

She was crying now. 'You believe me, then?' I asked her.

'Oh, yes, I do! I must take Flora far away, far from *them*!' she said.

'My letter — it will arrive in town first,' I said.

She shook her head. 'No, it won't. It's disappeared.'

'What do you mean?'

'It disappeared from the table by the front door. The other servants haven't seen it. Miles —'

'Miles took it?' This was terrible. 'Then he's read it! So he's a thief — he was stealing letters at school, then! I must talk to him. If he talks to me, we can save him!'

The servants were surprised when Flora left with Mrs Grose. They stared at me silently when I walked through the house. But Miles did not seem worried. We ate lunch together in the large dining-room.

'Is Flora very ill?' he asked me.

'She'll get better in London. Take some meat, Miles,' I said.

He filled his plate, and we ate quickly. Miles got up, and stood with his back to me and his hands in his little pockets. We did not speak while the servant took the plates away.

'Flora is saying such terrible things. Dreadful words, dreadful things.'

'Well,' Miles said. 'We're alone now!'

'Not quite alone,' I answered.

'Of course, there are the others,' he said. 'But they're not important, are they?' He walked to the window and put his face against the glass. Was he looking for something, or somebody?

'Have you enjoyed yourself today?' I asked.

'Oh, yes! I'm so free now. I walked miles and miles. I went everywhere.'

'And do you like it?'

'Do you?' he replied. '*You* are more alone now.'

'It doesn't matter,' I said. 'I'm happy to be here. And why am I still here? For you, of course.'

He stared at me, and his little face was both handsome and serious.

'You're staying here just for me?'

'Yes. I'm your friend, and I want to help you – I told you so, that night, in your bedroom. Do you remember?'

'Yes, but you wanted something from me, too!'

'Yes. Tell me everything, Miles. That's what I want!'

'Ah! You're staying here so that I can tell you everything!'

'Well, yes, it's true.'

'Now?' he asked.

'It's a good time. Or do you want to go out again?'

'Yes, I want to go out very much!' He picked up his hat, and was ready to leave. 'I'll tell you everything – I promise. But later – not now.'

'Why not now?'

He turned to the window again and was silent. 'I have to see the gardener,' he said. He was lying, I knew it. Someone was waiting for him outside.

'Well, then,' I said. 'Tell me just one little thing before you go. Did you take my letter from the table by the door?'

'Well,' Miles said. 'We're alone now!'

Then, in that same second, I saw the terrible face of Peter Quint at the window again. The room changed, and everything felt bad. But Miles saw nothing.

'Yes, I took it,' he said.

I took him in my arms. He could not see the ghost, and he was not lying now! These were two good, good things! The face still stared at us through the glass.

'Why did you take it?'

'I wanted to know what you wrote about me,' he said.

'And did you open the letter?' I asked.

'I opened it, and then I burnt it,' he said.

'And did you do this at school? Did you steal letters, and burn them? Did you steal other things, Miles?'

'*Me*?' he asked. '*Steal*?' His voice told me that this was a terrible question.

My face was red. 'Well, why can't you go back? What did you do, then?'

'I – I said things,' the boy replied, 'to a few people. And then all the masters heard about it. That's all.'

'What things?' I asked. But he didn't say. Perhaps he really was innocent!

'Didn't they tell you? Well, there *were* some bad things. Perhaps they were too bad for a letter.'

But the face at the window came closer. It wanted to stop Miles, to stop his true answers. I screamed and held Miles again. 'No more, no more!' I shouted to the ghost.

'Is *she* here?' Miles asked, and turned his eyes to the window. But he could still see nothing.

'She?' I asked.

'Miss Jessel, Miss Jessel!' he shouted in anger.

I understood then; he was thinking about Flora's story.

'No, it's not Miss Jessel. But that other dreadful face – that wicked man – he's at the window *for the last time*!'

*I saw the terrible face of Peter Quint at the window again . . .
But Miles saw nothing.*

*I realised what I was holding. I was holding a dead child, not a living one.*

He got angrier then, and the room felt worse. '*He* is here then?' he asked.

'Who?' I had to ask him.

'Peter Quint, of course! Where is he?' He looked round the room. 'Where?'

'It doesn't matter!' I said. 'I have you now! You are mine, not his! He has lost you for ever! There, there!' I pointed. But Miles saw nothing. He screamed like an animal, like a person who has lost everything. 'He's falling!' I thought. 'I must catch him and save him!' I held him hard, very hard. And then Miles and I were alone, alone together in a quiet afternoon. But suddenly, his little heart stopped, and I realised what I was holding. I was holding a dead child, not a living one.

# ACTIVITIES

## Chapters 1–3

*Before you read*
1  Do you think that this story will be happy, sad or frightening? Why do you think so?
2  Find these words in your dictionary. They are all in this part of the story.

   alone   dreadful   employ   ghost   governess   innocence
   lady   master   naughty   servant   stare   tower

   **a**  Which words mean the same as the following:
   - to look at something for a long time
   - a tall, narrow building
   - without other people
   - a woman who teaches young children in their home
   - a person who comes back after he or she is dead

   **b**  Choose the right words from the list above and put them in these sentences:
   - The factory now ..... more than 200 workers.
   - One child is good but the other is very ......
   - The man was not a criminal: he was able to prove his ......
   - The dog always comes when its ..... calls its name.
   - This beautiful ..... is married to a very rich man.
   - Rich people usually have ..... to cook their meals.
   - There has been a ..... accident in Oxford Road.

*After you read*
3  What are the names of these people?
   **a**  the housekeeper at the big house
   **b**  the child with gold hair
   **c**  the beautiful boy
   **d**  the man with the strange eyes
4  Answer these questions:
   **a**  Who shows the governess round the house and garden?
   **b**  Why does the head at Miles's school want Miles to leave the school?

**c** Where is the strange man when the governess first sees him?
   **d** What is he doing the second time she sees him?
   **e** How do we know that he is a ghost?

## Chapters 4–6

*Before you read*
 5 Find these words in your dictionary. They are all in this part of the story.
   *candle   suffer   wicked*
   Which word means:
   **a** to feel great pain
   **b** a simple kind of light
   **c** very, very bad
 6 Answer these questions:
   **a** What do you think that Peter Quint wants?
   **b** Can you name all the people in the pictures for these three chapters?

*After you read*
 7 Who says these words? Who are they talking to?
   **a** 'She was a lady and he was only a servant.'
   **b** 'You were crying.'
   **c** 'I wanted to be bad.'
   **d** 'You're a wicked, terrible woman!'
   **e** 'I cannot teach a boy who is wicked.'

## Chapters 7–8

*Before you read*
 8 In these last two chapters one person dies. Who do you think it will be?
 9 Who will win in the end: the good people or the ghosts?

*After you read*
 10 The governess writes a letter. What happens to it?
 11 At the end of Chapter 7, the governess cries for a long time. Why is she crying?

**12** At the end of the story, Peter Quint returns. He wants to stop Miles – from doing what?

**Writing**

**13** Write five things you know about Flora: what she looks like etc.
**14** In Chapter 6, the governess writes a letter to her employer. What do you think she says? Write the letter.
**15** Think of a ghost story you know. Write a paragraph telling the story.
**16** You are a scientist: you don't believe in ghosts. Explain that the governess imagined everything. Give another reason why Miles dies at the end of the story.

---

Answers for the Activities in this book are published in our free resource packs for teachers, the Penguin Readers Factsheets, or available on a separate sheet. Please write to your local Pearson Education office or to: Marketing Department, Penguin Longman Publishing, 5 Bentinck Street, London W1M 5RN.

# *Jane Eyre*

## CHARLOTTE BRONTË

Level 3

Retold by Ann Ward
Series Editors: Andy Hopkins and Jocelyn Potter

## Contents

| | page |
|---|---|
| Introduction | 189 |
| Jane Eyre | 193 |
| Activities | 230 |

# *Introduction*

*Someone was in my room. It was a woman. She was a big woman, tall and strong. At first I did not see her face. She looked at herself in the mirror. Then I saw her face! It was the most terrible face. She looked angry, cruel and frightening.*

Jane Eyre works for Mr Rochester. He owns a large country house, Thornfield Hall, and there Jane teaches a little French girl, Adèle. But Jane also loves Mr Rochester. Does Rochester love her? Is Jane right to love him?

Rochester is very rich, and Jane is poor. But more important than that, Thornfield Hall holds a terrible secret. Only Rochester knows what it is – and he will say nothing . . .

Charlotte Brontë was born in 1816 in a village in Yorkshire, in the north of England. The family soon moved to a nearby village called Haworth. Her father was the village clergyman and their house was next to the church. Her mother died when Charlotte was five years old. An aunt came to look after the six children. In 1824 the four oldest sisters, Maria, Elizabeth, Charlotte and Emily, went away to school. The school was a cold, unhappy place, and the girls did not have enough to eat. Maria and Elizabeth became ill and died. This is the school that Charlotte later describes as Lowood in *Jane Eyre*. After that, Charlotte, her two younger sisters and her brother Branwell had their lessons at home. They began to write stories together. They called their stories *The Gondal Chronicles*. Some of these writings still exist. Charlotte was now the oldest. She spent three years away from home teaching in a school, and then she lived with two local families as a teacher to their children.

In 1842 Charlotte and Emily went to Belgium to study French. They returned home when their aunt died but Charlotte went back to Brussels the next year to continue her studies. She was now in love with M. Heger, whose wife owned the language school where Charlotte was studying. But there was no hope for Charlotte: lonely and unhappy, she returned home once more.

The three sisters, Charlotte, Emily and Anne, continued to write. In 1846, they decided to bring out a book of poems, using the names Currer, Ellis and Acton Bell. They found a company to take their work but it sold very few copies of the *Poems*. The sisters then each tried to sell stories to the book company. Anne sent *Agnes Grey* and Emily sent *Wuthering Heights*. Both books came out in 1847. Charlotte sent *The Professor*, a story about a young woman and a Belgian teacher, but the book company did not like it. She then sent *Jane Eyre*, and this story came out that same year, 1847. It was an immediate success. Suddenly everybody wanted to meet Currer, Ellis and Acton Bell. Charlotte was now famous but terrible unhappiness followed. Her brother and sisters all died: Branwell in September 1848, Emily in December of the same year and Anne the next March.

Charlotte continued to write. *Shirley* (1849) is a story set in Yorkshire. It is about the lives of men and women factory workers and their cruel employers. *Villette* (1853), set in Belgium, uses much of the same subject matter as *The Professor* but most readers agree that it is a much better story. *The Professor*, her first book, came out only in 1857, after Charlotte's death, and many people find it the weakest of her works.

Charlotte received many offers of marriage. She finally chose a young clergyman, her father's assistant. They married in 1854 but Charlotte died in March of the next year. After her death, her father, Patrick Brontë, asked Mrs Gaskell, another well-known writer, to write the story of Charlotte's life. This book, *The Life of Charlotte Brontë* (1857), made her even more famous.

*Jane Eyre* remains Charlotte Brontë's best known book. Jane is a good-hearted person with a strong sense of right and wrong. But she also has deep feelings. The many difficulties she faces do not shake her love for the mysterious Mr Rochester. *Jane Eyre* is one of the world's greatest love stories.

*John picked up a large, heavy book and threw it straight at me.*

# Jane Eyre

My name is Jane Eyre and my story begins when I was ten. I was living with my aunt, Mrs Reed, because my mother and father were both dead. Mrs Reed was rich. Her house was large and beautiful, but I was not happy there. Mrs Reed had three children, Eliza, John and Georgiana. My cousins were older than I. They never wanted to play with me and they were often unkind. I was afraid of them.

I was most afraid of my cousin John. He enjoyed frightening me and making me feel unhappy. One afternoon, I hid from him in a small room. I had a book with a lot of pictures in it and I felt quite happy. John and his sisters were with their mother.

But then John decided to look for me.

'Where's Jane Eyre?' he shouted, 'Jane! Jane! Come out!' He could not find me at first – he was not quick or clever. But then Eliza, who was clever, found my hiding place.

'Here she is!' she shouted. I had to come out. And John was waiting for me.

'What do you want?' I asked him.

'I want you to come here,' John said. I went and stood in front of him. He looked at me for a long time, and then suddenly he hit me. 'Now go and stand near the door!' he said.

I was very frightened. I knew that John wanted to hurt me. I went and stood near the door. Then John picked up a large, heavy book and threw it straight at me. The book hit me on the head and I fell.

'You cruel boy!' I shouted. 'You always want to hurt me. Look!' I touched my head. There was blood on it.

John became angrier. He ran across the room and started to hit me again and again. I was hurt and afraid, so I hit him back.

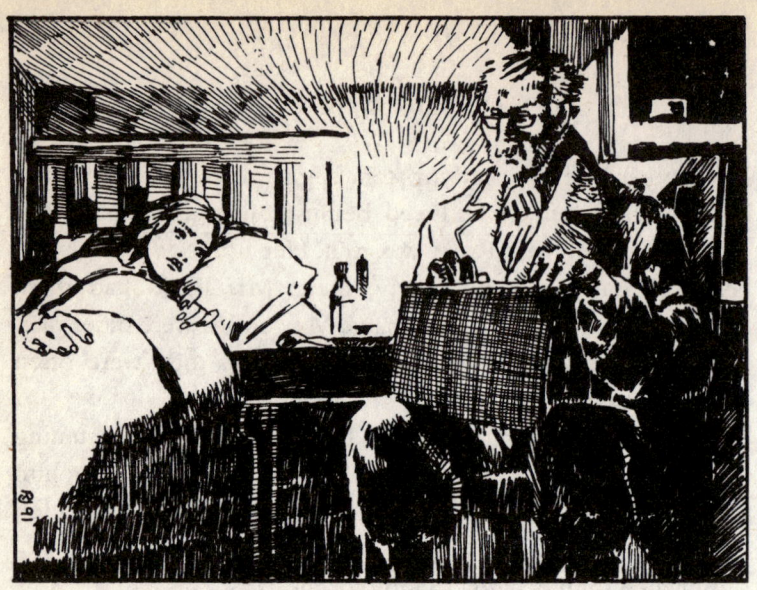

*When at last I woke up, I was in my bed. The doctor was there. 'What happened?' I asked him.*

Mrs Reed heard the noise and hurried into the room. She was very angry. She did not seem to notice the blood on my head.

'Jane Eyre! You bad girl!' she shouted. 'Why are you hitting your poor cousin? Take her away! Take her to the red room and lock the door!'

The red room was cold and dark. I was very frightened. Nobody ever went into the red room at night. I cried for help, but nobody came. 'Please help me!' I called, 'Don't leave me here!'

But nobody came to open the door. I cried for a long time, and then everything suddenly went black. I remember nothing after that.

When at last I woke up, I was in my bed. My head was hurting. The doctor was there. 'What happened?' I asked him.

'You are ill, Jane,' the doctor answered. 'Tell me, Jane. Are you unhappy here with your aunt and your cousins?'

'Yes, I am,' I answered. 'I'm very unhappy.'

'I see,' said the doctor. 'Would you like to go away to school?' he asked.

'Oh, yes, I think so,' I told him. The doctor looked at me again, and then he left the room. He talked to Mrs Reed for a long time. They decided to send me away to school.

So not long afterwards, I left my aunt's house to go to school. Mrs Reed and my cousins were pleased when I went away. I was not really sad to leave. 'Perhaps I'll be happy at school,' I thought. 'Perhaps I'll have some friends there.'

♦

One night in January, after a long journey, I arrived at Lowood School. It was dark and the weather was cold, windy and rainy.

The school was very large, but it was not warm and comfortable, like Mrs Reed's house. A teacher took me into a big room. It was full of girls. There were about eighty girls there. The youngest girls were nine, and the eldest were about twenty. They all wore ugly brown dresses.

It was supper time. There was water to drink, and a small piece of bread to eat. I was thirsty, and drank some water. I could not eat anything because I felt too tired and too excited. After supper, all the girls went upstairs to bed. The teacher took me into a very long room. All the girls slept in this room. Two girls had to sleep in each bed.

Early in the morning, I woke up. It was still dark outside and the room was very cold. The girls washed themselves in cold water and put on their brown dresses. Then everybody went downstairs and the early morning lessons began.

*A teacher took me into a big room. It was full of girls. There were about eighty girls there.*

At last, it was time for breakfast. I was now very hungry. We went into the dining-room with the teachers. There was a terrible smell of burning food. We were all hungry, but when we tasted the food we could not eat it. It tasted terrible. Feeling very hungry, we all left the dining-room.

At nine o'clock, lessons began again. I looked round at the other girls. They looked very strange in their ugly brown dresses. I did not like the teachers. They seemed to be unkind and unfriendly.

Then at twelve o'clock, the head teacher, Miss Temple, came in. She was very pretty and her face was kind. 'I want to speak to all the girls,' she said. 'I know that you could not eat your breakfast this morning,' she told us. 'So now you will have some bread and cheese and a cup of coffee.' The other teachers looked surprised. 'I'll pay for this meal,' Miss Temple said. The girls were very pleased.

After this meal, we went out into the garden. The girls' brown dresses were too thin for the cold winter weather. Most of the girls looked cold and unhappy, and some of them looked very ill. I walked around and looked at the girls and at the school and the garden. But I did not speak to anyone, and nobody spoke to me.

One of the girls was reading a book. 'Is your book interesting?' I asked her.

'I like it,' she answered.

'Does this school belong to Miss Temple?' I asked.

'No, it doesn't,' she answered. 'It belongs to Mr Brocklehurst. He buys all our food and all our clothes.'

The girl's name was Helen Burns. She was older than I was. I liked her immediately. She became my friend.

Helen told me that many of the girls were ill because they were always cold and hungry. Mr Brocklehurst was not a kind man. The clothes he bought for the girls were not warm enough for the winter, and there was never enough food to eat.

*I went to Miss Temple's room. Helen Burns was lying there in a little bed. She was now very thin, and her face was white.*

After a few months, many of the girls at Lowood School became seriously ill. Lessons stopped, and I and the other girls who were not ill spent all our time out in the fields near the school. The weather was now warm and sunny. It was a happy time for us, but my friend Helen Burns was not with us. She had to stay in bed. She was very ill.

One evening, I went to Miss Temple's room. Helen Burns was lying there in a little bed. She was now very thin, and her face was white. She spoke to me in a low voice. 'Jane,' she said, 'it's good to see you. I want to say goodbye to you.'

'Why?' I asked her. 'Are you going away?'

'Yes, I am,' Helen answered. 'I'm going far away.'

That night she died.

During that summer, many other girls in the school died too. Mr Brocklehurst sold the school, and it became a happier place.

I stayed at the school until I was eighteen and then I had to find a job. I wanted to become a teacher.

I wrote a letter to a newspaper. I said I was a young teacher, who wanted a job working in a family. Then I waited for an answer. At last, an answer came. It was from a lady, Mrs Fairfax, who lived at a place called Thornfield Hall. She needed a teacher for a little girl. So I packed my clothes in a small bag and travelled to Thornfield Hall.

♦

I felt very excited when I arrived at Thornfield Hall. The house was large, but it seemed very quiet. Mrs Fairfax met me at the door. She was an old lady with a kind face.

'Sit down, Miss Eyre,' she said. 'You look tired after your journey. Later, you will meet Adèle.'

'Is Adèle my student?' I asked.

'Yes, she is. She is French. Mr Rochester wants you to teach her English.'

'Who is Mr Rochester?' I asked.

Mrs Fairfax looked surprised. 'Did you not know? Thornfield Hall belongs to Mr Rochester,' she answered. 'I only work for him.'

'Is Mr Rochester here now?' I asked.

'No. He is away. He does not come very often to Thornfield. I do not know when he will return.'

Later, I met Adèle. She was a pretty little girl. I spoke to her in French, and began to teach her English. She enjoyed her lessons, and I enjoyed teaching her. I liked Adèle and I liked Mrs Fairfax, too. It was quiet at Thornfield Hall, and sometimes I felt a little bored, but everybody was kind to me there.

One afternoon, I walked to the village to post a letter. It was winter, and there was ice on the road. As I was walking back to Thornfield Hall, I heard a noise behind me. It was a horse. A man was riding towards Thornfield Hall. I stood on one side and the horse went past. The man did not see me. He was a stranger with dark hair. Suddenly, with a loud noise, the stranger's horse fell down on the ice. The man was lying on the ground, trying to get up. I ran forward to help.

'Are you hurt, sir?' I asked him.

The stranger looked surprised to see me. 'A little,' he answered. 'Could you help me to catch my horse? That's right. Now could you bring the horse here, please? Thank you.' The stranger tried to stand up, but his leg was hurting too much. He looked at me again. 'Could you help me to get up on its back again? Good. Thank you, Miss.'

I watched him as he rode away. 'Who is he?' I asked myself. 'He is not handsome, but he has an interesting face. I would like to know him.'

When I got back to Thornfield, everybody was very excited. Mrs Fairfax was very busy. 'What's happening?' I asked her.

'Oh, Miss Eyre,' said Mrs Fairfax, 'it is Mr Rochester! He has suddenly come back! But he will probably go away again soon. Now, Miss Eyre, you must go and put on your best dress. Mr Rochester wants to meet you and Adèle after dinner.'

Later that evening, I took Adèle to Mr Rochester's room. I felt rather afraid of meeting Mr Rochester. I went quietly into the room and saw a man there. I knew him. It was the man on the horse. So the interesting stranger was Mr Rochester!

Mr Rochester did not go away again. He was busy every day but sometimes in the evenings he talked to me. He was usually serious, and he did not smile or laugh very often, but he was

*A man was riding towards Thornfield Hall. Suddenly, with a loud noise, the stranger's horse fell down on the ice.*

*Mr Rochester was asleep and the bed was on fire! Quickly, I took some water and threw it all over the bed.*

interesting and I was not afraid of him. I began to enjoy myself more at Thornfield Hall.

♦

One night, I woke up suddenly. It was about two o'clock in the morning. I thought I heard a sound. Everything was very quiet. I listened carefully and the sound came again. Someone was walking about outside my room.

'Who's there?' I called. Nobody answered. I felt cold and frightened. The house was silent. I tried to sleep again.

Then I heard a laugh. It was a terrible, cruel laugh! I listened. Someone was walking away, going up the stairs to the attic. What was happening? I decided to go and find Mrs Fairfax. I put on some clothes and left my room. The house was quiet now, but suddenly I could smell smoke. Something was burning! I ran to find out.

The smoke was coming from Mr Rochester's room. I ran into the room and looked around. Mr Rochester was asleep in his bed, and the bed was on fire! 'What can I do?' I thought. Quickly, I looked around the room. Luckily, there was some water in one corner. As quickly as I could, I took the water and threw it all over the bed. Mr Rochester woke up.

'What's happening?' he shouted. 'Jane! Is it you? What are you doing?'

'Mr Rochester,' I said, 'your bed is on fire! You must get up at once.'

He jumped out of bed. There was water everywhere and the fire was still smoking. 'Jane, you've saved me from the fire! How did you know about it? Why did you wake up?' Mr Rochester asked. I told him about the noise outside my door and the terrible laugh.

Mr Rochester looked serious and angry. 'I must go upstairs to the attic. Stay here and wait for me, please. Do not wake Mrs Fairfax.' He left the room and I waited for him.

At last, he came back. He was still looking very serious. 'You can go back to bed, now, Jane. Everything is all right now.'

'Who lives in the attic?' I asked Mrs Fairfax the next day.

'Only Grace Poole,' she answered. 'She is one of the servants. She is a strange woman.'

I remembered Grace Poole. She was a strange, silent woman, who did not often speak to the other servants. So perhaps it was Grace Poole who walked around the house late at night and laughed strangely outside the doors.

That evening, when Adèle finished her lessons, I went downstairs. Mrs Fairfax met me. 'Mr Rochester left the house early this morning,' she said. 'He is going to stay with his friends. I think he will stay with them for some weeks. I do not know when he will come back.'

For several weeks, the house was very quiet again. Mr Rochester stayed with his friends and I continued my lessons with Adèle. I did not hear the strange and terrible laugh at night again.

One day, Mrs Fairfax showed me a letter from Mr Rochester. 'He is coming back,' she said, 'and he is bringing a lot of visitors with him. I am going to be very busy getting everything ready. Miss Blanche Ingram is coming too. She is very beautiful.'

Mr Rochester and his friends arrived. The visitors were all rich, important people. Miss Blanche Ingram was among them. She was beautiful but very proud. Some of the visitors were nice to me, but the others did not notice me. I was too poor and unimportant. Miss Ingram never spoke to me. She was not interested in me, but she seemed to be interested in Mr Rochester. She always seemed to enjoy her conversations with him. They often went out riding together.

'I think Mr Rochester will marry Miss Ingram,' said Mrs Fairfax.

But was Mr Rochester interested in Blanche Ingram? He seemed to like her, but he did not look very happy when they were together.

♦

One evening, a new visitor came to Thornfield Hall. He was a quiet young man with dark hair called Mr Mason. He came to see Mr Rochester on business. Mr Mason told us that he and Mr Rochester were old friends, but Mr Rochester was not very pleased to see Mr Mason. When Mr Rochester heard the name 'Mr Mason, from the West Indies', he was surprised and his face turned white.

*Blanche Ingram seemed to be interested in Mr Rochester. They often went out riding together.*

That night, Mr Rochester and Mr Mason talked for a long time. At last, very late at night, they went to bed. Soon, everyone in the house was asleep. Suddenly, I woke up. I heard a terrible scream from somewhere over my head. Then everything was very quiet again. I listened carefully, and then I heard a lot of noise from above my head. There seemed to be fighting in the room above. Then there was another scream.

'Help! Help!' someone shouted. There was more fighting. Then a voice called out 'Rochester! Come quickly! Help me!'

A door opened, and I heard someone running up the stairs to the attic. I quickly put on some clothes and opened my door. Everybody in the house was awake now. The visitors were all standing outside their doors.

'What's happening? Is there a fire? What was that noise?' they asked.

Mr Rochester came down from the attic. 'Please don't worry,' he told his friends. 'Everything is all right.'

'But what's happening?' somebody asked.

'One of the servants had a bad dream and started to scream,' Mr Rochester said. 'But everything is all right now. Please go back to bed.'

Slowly, all Mr Rochester's visitors returned to their rooms. I too went back to my room, but I did not go back to bed. I sat and looked out of the window. The house was very quiet now. There were no sounds from the attic.

Then someone knocked on my door. I opened it. Mr Rochester stood outside. 'Jane, come with me please,' he told me, 'but come quietly . . . follow me.'

I followed Mr Rochester up to the attic. He unlocked the door of a room and we went inside.

'Wait here,' Mr Rochester told me. I stood next to the door.

There was another door on the opposite side of the room. From behind this door I could hear a terrible sound. It was like an angry animal. Mr Rochester left me and went through this door. Once again, I heard that terrible, cruel laugh! Was Grace Poole behind the door? Mr Rochester spoke to someone inside the room, and then came out and locked the door again.

'Come here, Jane,' he told me quietly. I came further into the room. There was a large bed in the room. Mr Mason was lying on the bed. His face was white and his eyes were closed. There was a lot of blood on his shirt. He did not move.

'Is he dead?' I asked.

'No,' answered Mr Rochester. 'He isn't badly hurt but I must go and bring the doctor for him. Will you stay with him until I get back?'

The man on the bed moved, and tried to speak. Mr Rochester turned to him. 'Don't try to talk, Mason. Jane, do not speak to him, please. There must be no conversation between you.'

Mr Rochester hurried out of the room. I waited for him with the silent man on the bed. I was frightened. I knew that Grace Poole was in the next room. For a long time, I waited for Mr Rochester to return. 'When will he come back?' I asked myself.

At last morning came and Mr Rochester returned with the doctor. While the doctor was looking after Mr Mason, Mr Rochester spoke to me. 'Thank you for all your help, Jane. Mason is going to leave Thornfield Hall now. The doctor will take him away,' he told me.

We helped Mr Mason down the stairs and out of the house. It was still early, and the other people in the house were still asleep.

'Take care of poor Mason,' said Mr Rochester to the doctor. 'Soon he will be able to go back home to the West Indies.'

Before he left, Mr Mason said something very strange. 'Look after her, Rochester,' he said. 'Promise to look after her.'

*I waited for Mr Rochester's return with the silent man on the bed. I was frightened, I knew that Grace Poole was in the next room.*

Mr Rochester looked sad. 'I promise. I will always look after her.'

I started to go back to the house. 'Don't go, Jane,' said Mr Rochester. 'Come into the garden. Talk to me.'

We went into the garden. 'What a night!' he said. 'Were you frightened, Jane?'

'Yes, I was frightened. Up there, in the next room . . . there was someone . . . that terrible laugh . . . Mr Rochester, will Grace Poole go away now?'

'No,' he replied. 'But don't worry about Grace Poole. Try to forget about her. She isn't dangerous. It is Mason I am worrying about.'

I was surprised to hear this. 'Mr Mason? But he is frightened. He can't hurt you.'

Mr Rochester looked sad. 'I know Mason does not want to hurt me, but he could say something that will hurt me. I shall be happier when he goes back to the West Indies.'

♦

Later that day, I got a surprising letter. Mrs Reed, my aunt, was dying and she wanted to see me. It was a long journey to her home. When I got there, I heard that my cousin John was dead. Mrs Reed was very ill. At first, she did not want to speak to me. Then one day, when I was sitting by her bed, she showed me a letter. It was from my uncle, my father's brother, who lived in Madeira. This was the letter:

> *Dear Mrs Reed,*
> *Please help me. I want to find my brother's daughter, Jane Eyre. I am a rich man and I have no children. I want Jane Eyre to come and live with me.*
>
> *Yours sincerely,*
> *John Eyre.*

I read the letter and looked at the date on it. 'But, Mrs Reed,' I said, 'this is an old letter. You got it three years ago!'

'I know,' she said, 'but I never liked you, Jane Eyre. After I read the letter, I wrote to your uncle. I told him you were dead. I told him you died at Lowood School. Now go away! Leave me!'

Soon afterwards, Mrs Reed died, and I returned to Thornfield Hall. It was summer, and the fields around Thornfield Hall were very quiet and beautiful. For me, it was the most beautiful place in the world. It was my home now.

'Adèle will be pleased to see me,' I thought. 'But what about Mr Rochester? He is the person I most want to see. But does he want to see me? Perhaps by now he is already married to Blanche Ingram. If they are not already married, they will be married very soon.' I felt sad when I thought about Mr Rochester and Blanche Ingram. 'So I must soon leave this beautiful place,' I thought. 'I can't stay here when Mr Rochester is married. I will never see Thornfield Hall again. And worse than that, I will never see Mr Rochester again.'

As I came near the house, I met Mr Rochester. When I saw that he looked pleased to see me, I felt happier. Adèle and Mrs Fairfax were happy to see me too. 'The visitors have all left now,' said Mrs Fairfax. 'It is very quiet here. It is good to see you again.'

'Yes, this is my home,' I thought. 'I've always been happy here. How can I leave it?'

I started to work, teaching Adèle again. Everything was the same as before. Mr Rochester still said nothing about getting married to Blanche Ingram. Then one evening, he saw me in the garden. 'Come and talk to me, Jane,' he said.

I went towards him. 'Now,' I thought, 'he's going to tell me that he is going to get married.'

'Are you happy here, Jane?' he asked.

'Yes, I am, very happy,' I answered.

'And you like Adèle and Mrs Fairfax?'

'Very much,' I said.

'You'll be sad to leave them,' he said.

I looked away. 'Now he is going to tell me that I must leave because he is going to be married,' I thought. I looked at him. 'Yes,' I answered, 'I will be very sad to leave.'

'But you must leave, you know,' Mr Rochester said.

'Must I? Must I leave soon?'

'Yes, soon.'

'Then you are going to get married.'

'Yes, I am going to get married. Adèle must go to school, and you must get a new job. I will find you one. Far from here.'

'Far from here?' I asked. 'But then I'll never see Thornfield Hall again, and . . . and I'll never see you again, Mr Rochester.'

'Oh, when you are far from here, you'll soon forget me,' he said.

'No,' I thought, 'you will forget me perhaps, but I will never forget you.'

'Never,' I answered him, at last. And I started to cry. I could not speak.

He watched me carefully, then at last he spoke again. 'Perhaps you do not need to go,' he said. 'Perhaps you can stay here when I am married?'

Did Mr Rochester think that I had no feelings? Did he not understand how I felt? Were my feelings so unimportant? I now felt angry.

'No,' I told him. 'I could never stay. I will not stay. Miss Ingram . . . Miss Ingram will be your wife. I know that I am not rich and beautiful like Miss Ingram. I am poor and unimportant.

*Mr Rochester wanted to marry me! He wanted me to be his wife!*

But I can still feel sadness. And if you marry Miss Ingram, I must leave here.'

Mr Rochester looked at me, and then he smiled. 'I don't want you to go, Jane. And I am not going to marry Miss Ingram. Don't get excited. I want you to stay here. It's you I want to marry.'

I could not believe him. 'Now you are laughing at me,' I said.

'No, I am not,' he answered. 'I want you to marry me, Jane. Will you marry me?'

He looked at me so seriously that at last I did believe him. Mr Rochester wanted to marry me! He wanted me to be his wife!

'Yes, I will marry you,' I answered.

'I will make you happy, Jane,' he said. 'No one will stop us,' he continued, with a strange, half-sad look. I could not understand that look, but I was too happy to be worried about it.

It grew dark. The wind began to blow, and it started to rain, so we walked together back to the house.

◆

My wedding day was only a month later. Two nights before the wedding, I was in bed, asleep. My wedding dress was in the room. It was a windy night. The wind made a strange sound. Suddenly, I woke up. There was a light in the room. I thought it was morning, but it was still dark outside.

Someone was in my room. Was it Mrs Fairfax? Was it Grace Poole? It was neither of them. It was a woman, but I did not know her. She was a big woman, tall and strong. Her black hair was long and thick. Her clothes were long and white. At first I did not see her face. She took my dress and held it in front of her. She looked at herself in the mirror. Then I saw her face!

It was the most terrible face! The woman's eyes were large and red and her face was purple. She looked angry, cruel and frightening.

Then she took my dress, and angrily tore it to pieces. She threw the pieces of the dress on the floor. Next, she went to the window, and looked out. Then she started to come towards my bed. I was so frightened that I could not move. I could not scream for help. I lay still in bed. 'Is she going to kill me?' I thought. But suddenly the light disappeared and the room went dark.

When I woke up, it was morning. The sun was shining. At once, I remembered that strange and frightening woman. Did it all really happen or was it a dream? Did she really come into my room in the middle of the night? Then I saw my wedding dress.

*'Jane, I think you had a bad dream, I think it was perhaps Grace Poole who really tore your dress.'*

It was lying on the floor, torn to pieces, I picked up the pieces of the dress. So it was all true! That terrible woman was real!

When I told Mr Rochester about the woman and showed him my dress, he looked very worried and was silent for a long time.

'Jane, I think you had a bad dream,' he said at last. 'I think it was perhaps Grace Poole who really tore your dress, but in your dream it was some stranger.'

I was not sure about this, but I said nothing. That night, the night before the wedding, I slept in Adèle's room.

My wedding day came, and we went to the church. But

the wedding did not happen. In the church, while the clergyman was speaking, someone threw open the doors at the back and shouted 'Stop the wedding! Mr Rochester cannot get married! He has got a wife already! He is married to my sister!'

Everybody in the church turned round to see the speaker. It was Mr Mason, the man from the West Indies. But who was his sister? How could Mr Rochester be married? I could not believe it. My heart turned to ice. I looked at Mr Rochester. His face was white and hard. But he did not say that Mr Mason was mistaken.

'But where is Mr Rochester's wife, your sister?' the clergyman asked Mr Mason. 'Where does she live?'

'She lives at Thornfield Hall,' answered Mr Mason. 'She is still alive. I saw her there last April.'

'At Thornfield Hall!' the clergyman said. 'But I know of no Mrs Rochester at Thornfield Hall. There must be some mistake.'

Mr Rochester was silent for a long time. 'I can explain,' he said at last. 'I'll tell you everything. It is true. My wife is living at Thornfield Hall. We got married fifteen years ago in the West Indies, when I was a young man. My wife's name was Bertha Mason. She is Mason's sister. Soon after the wedding, Bertha became very strange. Slowly, she became mad and dangerous. She wanted to kill me, and she tried to kill anybody who came near her. Last April, she tried to kill her brother, Mr Mason.'

'Nobody knows about Bertha, nobody knows that she is my wife. This young lady, Jane Eyre, knows nothing about her. A nurse, Grace Poole, looks after Bertha.' Mr Rochester's face was dark and serious. 'Come with me,' he said, 'now I will take you all to see her.'

We all left the church. Without speaking, we returned to Thornfield Hall. When we got there, Mr Rochester took us up to the attic. He took out a key and unlocked the door. Grace Poole was there, and in the room with her there was a

*Someone threw open the doors at the back of the church, and shouted 'Stop the wedding!'*

frightening woman, the terrible woman that I saw in my bedroom, the person with the cruel, mad laugh! She was the person who tried to kill Mr Mason and who set fire to Mr Rochester's room! She was mad. But she was Mr Rochester's wife and I could not marry him.

Poor Mr Rochester! I felt sorry for him. But I could not now stay at Thornfield Hall.

'I must leave my home for ever,' I thought, with a heavy heart. 'I can never come back and I will never see Mr Rochester again.'

Sadly, I put a few ordinary clothes into a small bag. I did not take my beautiful new clothes. I took a little money and quietly left Thornfield Hall early one morning. I did not say goodbye to anybody and nobody saw me leave.

♦

I wanted to travel as far away from Thornfield Hall as I could. I spent all my money. I travelled for two days and nights until at last I arrived at a place where there were no towns or villages and very few houses. I had no money now to buy food. I was very tired and very hungry.

It was evening and it was getting dark. I could see only one house. I went to the house and looked through the window. There were two young women in the room. They looked kind, so I knocked on the door. A servant opened it.

'Who are you?' she asked. 'What do you want?'

'I'm a stranger,' I said. 'I haven't any money or food. I'm tired and hungry. Please help me.'

The servant looked at me for a long time. 'I'll give you some bread,' she answered at last. 'But then you must go away.' She left me and came back with a piece of bread. 'Now go!' she said. 'You can't stay here.'

But I was too tired to move. I sat down on the ground by the door. 'Nobody will help me,' I said. 'I will die.'

*I did not know, but someone was listening and watching me.
'You won't die' he said.*

I did not know, but someone was listening and watching me.

'You won't die,' he said. 'Who are you?' I looked up and saw a tall young man. He knocked loudly on the door. The servant opened it again.

'Hannah,' the man asked, 'who is this young woman?'

'I don't know,' said the servant, Hannah. 'I told her to go away, but she's still here. Go away!' she said to me.

'No, Hannah, she can't go away. She is ill and she needs our help. She must come inside,' the man said.

They took me into the house. The room was warm. The two young women came to talk to me.

'What's your name?' they asked.

'My name's Jane Elliot,' I said. I did not want anyone to know my real name. I did not want Mr Rochester to find me. I wanted to start again.

My new friends gave me some food and took me to a bedroom where I slept for a long time.

After a few days I felt better, and was able to talk to my kind new friends. Their names were Diana and Mary Rivers. The man was their brother. His name was St John Rivers and he was a clergyman. St John was a very handsome young man with fair hair and blue eyes. He was always very serious. He did not often laugh or smile. He was planning to go to India to work.

His sisters were more friendly but I did not want to tell them about Mr Rochester. I thanked them for their kindness. 'I have no family,' I said. 'My parents are both dead. I was at Lowood School for six years. After that, I got a job with a family, but I had to leave suddenly. I didn't do anything wrong. Please believe me.'

'Don't talk now,' said Diana. 'You are tired.'

'You will want a new job now,' said St John.

'Yes,' I replied. 'As soon as possible.'

'Good. I will help you.'

A month later, Diana and Mary left their home to work as teachers in the south of England. St John asked me to teach the children who lived near his church. They were poor children and the school was very small. I was the only teacher.

I enjoyed my work. I did not have much money and I had to work very hard. I lived in a very small house near the school. There were not many people there, but St John was very kind and gave me books to read. In my free time, I read and painted pictures. Sometimes, St John visited me in the evenings.

One evening, he came to my house when I was just finishing a painting. He looked at some of my pictures. Then he looked again, more closely, at one of the paintings. Without saying anything, he tore a piece of paper off the bottom of the painting, and put it carefully into his pocket. Then, quite suddenly, he left. I was very surprised. What a strange person he was!

The next day it snowed. I thought no visitors would come that day. But in the evening there was a knock on the door. It was St John. He was wet and cold.

'Why have you come? Is there bad news?' I asked. 'Are your sisters all right?'

'Don't worry. There is no bad news. Diana and Mary are both well,' he answered. He sat down in front of the fire. I waited but he said nothing. 'How strange he is!' I thought. 'Why did he come here when the weather is so bad? Perhaps he is bored. His sisters are far away.'

St John sat and thought for a long time. At last, he spoke.

'I know your story,' St John said. 'I know about your parents, and about Mrs Reed. I know about Lowood School. And I know about Thornfield Hall and about Mr Rochester. I also know about Mr Rochester's wife. So now I know why you came here without any money. I know why you left Thornfield Hall. Mr Rochester must be a very bad man.'

'Oh, no. He isn't,' I said.

'I have had a letter,' said St John, 'from a man in London called Mr Briggs. He wants to find you. He asked about Jane Eyre. You call yourself Jane Elliot, but I know your real name is Jane Eyre. Look!' St John showed me a piece of paper. It was the piece of paper from the bottom of my painting. My real name, Jane Eyre, was on it.

'Did Mr Briggs say anything about Mr Rochester?' I asked. 'How is Mr Rochester?' I only wanted to know about Mr Rochester. I still loved him.

'Mr Briggs doesn't know anything about your Mr Rochester,' said St John. 'He wrote to me about your uncle, Mr Eyre of Madeira. Your uncle is dead. He has left you all his money. You are a very rich young woman.'

For a long time, I was too surprised to speak. I was rich now, but I was not excited. I tried to understand what it meant to be rich.

'I can't understand,' I said at last. 'Why did Mr Briggs write to you?'

'Because,' St John said, 'Mr Eyre of Madeira was also our uncle. He was my mother's brother. When he died, he left all his money to you, Jane Eyre.'

'Then you, Diana and Mary are my cousins!' I said. 'This is wonderful news! Our uncle's money is for all of us. Diana and Mary can come home, and we can all live together.' It was good to have money, but it was even better to have three cousins.

So, just before Christmas, Diana and Mary came home. I worked hard to make their old house comfortable. 'Diana and Mary will like it,' I thought. 'But what about St John? He's a strange man. He's like stone, hard and cold. He's pleased to see his sisters, but still he does not really look happy.'

Diana, Mary and I began to live quietly and comfortably together. St John still wanted to go to India. I was happy living with my cousins but I still thought about Mr Rochester every day. Where was he? Was he happy? I wrote to the lawyer, Mr Briggs, but Mr Briggs knew nothing about Mr Rochester. Then I wrote to Mrs Fairfax at Thornfield Hall. I waited for a letter from her, but no letter came. I wrote to Mrs Fairfax again; perhaps she did not get my first letter. Again there was no answer. At last, a letter did come for me, but it was only a letter from Mr Briggs about my uncle's money. I began to cry.

While I was crying, St John came into the room and saw me. 'Jane,' he said, 'come for a walk with me. No, don't call Diana and Mary. I want to talk to you.'

We walked along the side of the river. At first, St John said nothing. At last, he turned to me. 'Jane, I'm going to India in six weeks and I want you to come with me.'

I was surprised. Why did St John want me to go to India with him? How could I help him? I was not strong and serious like him.

'As your helper?' I asked. 'I don't think . . .'

'No, not as my helper. As my wife. I want to marry you, so that we can work together in India. There are many poor people there. They need our help.'

Now I was even more surprised. I felt sure that St John did not love me. And I did not want to marry him. I could not marry him. I still loved Mr Rochester.

'But I can't go to India,' I said. 'I don't know how to help the people there. I'm not like you.'

St John looked at me seriously. 'Oh, that doesn't matter. I'll tell you what to do and you'll quickly learn. You always worked hard in the village school. You'll work hard in India, too.'

I thought for a long time. St John, my cousin, needed my help. He was going to do very useful work in India. At last, I continued. 'Perhaps I can help you, but I must be free. I cannot marry you. You're like my brother,' I said.

St John looked at me. His handsome face was cold and serious,

*I said 'Perhaps I can help you but I must be free. I cannot marry you. You're like my brother.'*

like stone. 'That's not possible. You must be my wife. I don't want a sister. I don't want you to marry another man. I want you to stay with me, to work with me, until we die.'

I felt cold and sad. I remembered my love for Mr Rochester and the way he always spoke to me. St John was different. He wanted me to marry him, but I knew he did not love me. I wanted to help him, but not to marry him. He was a good man, but I did not love him. I did not know what to say to him.

'I'm going away for two weeks,' St John continued. 'When I come back, I want your answer. I hope you will decide to marry me. You can't just stay here doing nothing.'

When I went back into the house, Diana spoke to me. 'Jane, you look unhappy. Your face is white. What is happening?'

I told her. 'St John asked me to marry him.'

'But that's wonderful!' she said. 'Now he will stay in England. He won't go to India. He'll stay here with us.'

'No,' I said, 'He wants me to go to India with him.'

'But you cannot go to India!' she said. 'You aren't strong enough.'

'I won't go,' I told her, 'because I can't marry St John. And now I'm afraid he's angry with me. He's a good man, but he doesn't understand how ordinary people feel.'

'I know,' Diana said. 'Our brother is a very good man, but he sometimes seems cold and hard.'

That night, I thought about St John for a long time. I did not know what to do. I did not love him, and he did not love me. But perhaps I could help him in India. I did not know what to do. The night was very quiet.

Suddenly, I thought I heard a voice. 'Jane! Jane! Jane!' it called. It was Mr Rochester's voice.

'Where are you?' I cried. But there was no answer. There was no one there. Was it only a dream? No, I knew that somewhere, far away, Mr Rochester needed me. 'I must go and find him,' I thought.

♦

The next day, I went to look for Mr Rochester. After a long journey, I arrived at Thornfield Hall. I walked for the last two miles to the house. I was excited; I was hurrying to see my old home again. The trees were the same, the road was the same. I arrived at the house and stopped . . . and stood and looked.

It was terrible! Where was Thornfield Hall, my beautiful home? No one could live here now. Now I understood why Mrs Fairfax never answered my letters. The walls of the house were still standing, but the windows were empty and dark and there was no roof. The grass was long and there were no flowers in the

*I arrived at the house and stopped . . . and stood and looked.
It was terrible! No one could live here now.*

garden. The broken walls of the Hall were black and silent. The only sounds were the birds and the wind. Where was Mrs Fairfax now? Where was little Adèle? And where was Mr Rochester?

I hurried back to the village to find out. I asked a man in the village to tell me about Thornfield Hall.

'No one lives there now,' he told me. 'Last autumn, Thornfield Hall burned down. It was terrible. The house burned down in the middle of the night.'

'How did it happen?' I asked him.

'They think Mr Rochester's wife started it. Nobody ever saw her, but people say she was mad. People think she started a fire in her room in the attic. When it happened, the house was almost empty. Mr Rochester was in the house, but the little girl, Adèle, was away at school and old Mrs Fairfax was staying with some friends, many miles away. It seems that Mr Rochester did not want to see anybody at that time. People say he seemed very unhappy. They say that he wanted to marry a young woman, but she ran away.'

'Tell me about the fire,' I said.

'When the fire started,' he continued, 'Mr Rochester got all the servants out of the house, then he went back in to save his wife. She was still in the attic. But she climbed up on to the roof. I saw her there. She stood on the roof, shouting and waving her arms. Mr Rochester tried to help her, but he could do nothing. Suddenly, she fell from the roof.'

'Did she die?' I asked.

'Yes, she did. She died immediately, and Mr Rochester was very badly hurt. He could not get out of the burning house in time. When at last he came out, he was blind, and he had lost one hand.' The man shook his head.

So Mr Rochester was still alive! He was hurt, but he was not dead. Suddenly, I began to hope again. I continued to question the man.

'Where does Mr Rochester live now?' I asked. 'Does he live in England?'

'Yes,' the man answered. 'He cannot travel far, poor man. He lives at Ferndean, about thirty miles from here. It is a quiet place. He lives there quietly with two servants. He never has any visitors.'

I decided to go to Ferndean at once. I arrived there just before dark. As I got near the house, the front door opened and a man came out. I knew at once it was Mr Rochester. But he was very different now. He was still tall and strong, and his hair was still black. But his face looked sad, and he could not walk without help. At last, he turned and went sadly back into the house.

The servant, Mary, who answered the door, knew me at once. She was very surprised to see me. I told her that I knew all about Mr Rochester and the fire at Thornfield Hall. 'Tell Mr Rochester that he has a visitor. But don't tell him who it is.'

'He won't see you, Miss Jane,' she said. 'He won't see anybody now.'

I went into the room.

'Who's there?' Mr Rochester asked. 'Is that you, Mary? Answer me! What's happening?'

'Will you have some water?' I asked him.

'Who's that? Tell me!' he said. He was surprised and excited.

'Mary knows me,' I said. 'I only came this evening.' I took his hand.

'Jane? Is it Jane?' he asked. 'Jane, is it really you?'

'Yes, it is,' I said. 'I'm so happy to be with you again. I'll never leave you now.'

'But Jane, where did you go? What happened to you? Why did you leave Thornfield Hall so suddenly? Why did you go away without any money? Why did you not stay and let me help you?' he asked.

'You know why I left,' I said. 'I am sorry you were worried.

But things are different now. I'm a rich woman,' I said. 'And I've got three cousins.' I told Mr Rochester all about my cousins and my new home.

'You do not need me now,' he said. 'But will you really stay with me?' There was hope in his voice again.

'Of course I will,' I said.

'But you're young. You'll want to get married some time. But not to me. I'm blind now and I can't do anything. You won't want to marry me. You'll want to marry some young man. What is your cousin, St John Rivers, like?' he asked. 'Is he an old man?'

'No. He is young and handsome.'

'Do you like him?' Mr Rochester asked.

'Yes, I do,' I answered. 'He's a very good man.'

'And does he like you?'

'Yes, I think so. He wants me to marry him.'

'And will you marry him?'

'No. I will not marry him. I do not love him.'

Mr Rochester looked suddenly happier. He took my hand. He was silent for a long time, and then he spoke. 'Jane, I can ask you again now: will you marry me?' he asked.

'Yes, I will,' I told him. At last, I felt really happy. And Mr Rochester, too, was no longer sad.

Three days later, I became Mr Rochester's wife.

I wrote to Diana and Mary. The news made them very happy. I also wrote to St John, but I had no answer from him. He went to India and continued to work very hard there. He never got married.

Mr Rochester and I are very happy together. We have been married for ten years now. Two years after we were married, Mr Rochester began to see again with one eye. He will never be able to see well, but he now can see me and he can see our children. Our story was a strange and sad one, and terrible things happened to us, but now at last we are happy together.

Then Mr Rochester spoke. 'Jane, I can ask you again now,' he said. 'Will you marry me?'

# ACTIVITIES

**Pages 193–205**

*Before you read*
1 Look at the pictures in this book. Which of the activities below can you see in them? Put 'yes' or 'no' beside each.

   a  riding
   b  playing the piano
   c  eating
   d  swimming
   e  sleeping
   f  falling
   g  writing a letter
   h  burning
   i  washing
   j  tearing a dress

2 These words come in this part of the story. Use a dictionary to learn their meaning.

   attic   cruel   pack   servant

   Now put each word in one of the sentences below.
   a  I must ..... my suitcase tonight because I am going abroad tomorrow.
   b  The room at the top of a house under the roof is called the ...... We keep things that we are not using there.
   c  Their house was very big and they needed three or four ..... to keep it clean.
   d  His wife is a kind person but he is very ......

*After you read*
3 What are their names?
   a  Jane's cruel cousin?
   b  Jane's aunt
   c  the head teacher
   d  the owner of the school
   e  Jane's schoolfriend
   f  Jane's student

4 Answer these questions:
   a  Why is Jane living with her aunt?
   b  Who helps Jane to leave her aunt's house? How?

5 Correct these sentences about Lowood School:
   a  The building was warm and comfortable.
   b  The girls wore warm, pretty clothes.
   c  There were about 100 girls at the school.

**d** There was plenty of good food at meal-times.
  **6** At Thornfield Hall, Jane wakes one night at two in the morning. What does she
  **a** hear  **b** smell  **c** see?
  What does she do then?

## Pages 206–217

*Before you read*
  **7** Choose the right answer.
  **a** A *clergyman* is a   (i)   musician
                             (ii)  scientist
                             (iii) man of the church
  **b** *Mad* means:         (i)   crazy
                             (ii)  lonely
                             (iii) clever
  **8** Mr Rochester is much older than Jane. Does a big difference in age between husband and wife matter in a marriage? Talk about this with other students.

*After you read*
  **9** Answer these questions:
  **a** What really happens during the night that Mr Mason comes to stay?
  **b** When Mr Mason says goodbye, he also says something which Jane thinks is 'very strange'. What does he say? Who is he talking about?
  **c** Mr Rochester says: 'I know Mason does not want to hurt me but he could say something that will hurt me.' Later, his words come true. How?
  **10** Who says these words? Who to?
  **a** 'When you are far from here, you'll soon forget me.'
  **b** 'I am poor and unimportant but I can still feel sadness.'
  **c** 'He has got a wife already! He is married to my sister!'

**Pages 218–229**

*Before you read*

11  Choose the right answer.
    **a** A person who is *blind*
        (i) is not very clever
        (ii) cannot see
        (iii) is left-handed
    **b** A *lawyer* is
        (i) a person who has studied law
        (ii) somebody who does not break the law
        (iii) a person who makes laws

*After you read*

12  Answer these questions:
    **a** Who are Jane's new friends?
    **b** How does St John learn Jane's real surname?
13  Put these parts of the story in the right order:
    **a** Mrs Rochester falls from the roof and dies.
    **b** Mr Rochester moves to Ferndean.
    **c** Thornfield Hall catches fire and burns down.
    **d** Jane decides to go back to Thornfield Hall.
    **e** Mr Rochester becomes blind.

## Writing

14  Write a short description of one of these people:
    **a** John Reed  **b** Blanche Ingram  **c** St John Rivers
    Use pictures in the book to help you.
15  You are St John Rivers. You have not forgotten Jane. Write her a letter from India, repeating your offer of marriage.
16  You are making a film of *Jane Eyre*. Which film stars do you choose to play the people in the story? Why?
17  Did you enjoy this book or not? Write a short report for other students to read. Say what the book is about and which parts you enjoyed most.

---

Answers for the Activities in this book are published in our free resource packs for teachers, the Penguin Readers Factsheets, or available on a separate sheet. Please write to your local Pearson Education office or to: Marketing Department, Penguin Longman Publishing, 5 Bentinck Street, London W1M 5RN.

# Sense and Sensibility

## JANE AUSTEN

Level 3

Retold by Cherry Gilchrist
Series Editors: Andy Hopkins and Jocelyn Potter

## *Contents*

|  |  | page |
|---|---|---|
| Introduction | | 236 |
| Chapter 1 | A New Home | 239 |
| Chapter 2 | An Invitation to Dinner | 242 |
| Chapter 3 | The Handsome Stranger | 243 |
| Chapter 4 | A Secret Engagement | 248 |
| Chapter 5 | An Unkind Letter | 254 |
| Chapter 6 | A Family Disagreement | 261 |
| Chapter 7 | All's Well That Ends Well | 266 |
| Activities | | 278 |

# Introduction

*Marianne forgot about Colonel Brandon, but he did not forget about her. Elinor liked him and was sorry for him, but what could she do? Can a quiet gentleman of thirty-five win against a handsome young one of twenty-five?*

Mrs Dashwood and her daughters must leave Norland, their family home, and move to a small house in another part of the country. They have very little money now and must live more simply. But almost at once, Marianne, the middle daughter, meets a handsome young stranger called Willoughby. Soon everybody thinks that they will marry. Elinor, her older sister, is more serious. She loves a quiet, sensible young man called Edward Ferrars. But Willoughby suddenly leaves for London, and Edward doesn't seem interested in Elinor now. What has gone wrong?

Jane Austen, one of England's greatest novelists, was born in 1775 in Hampshire, in the south of England. Her father was a priest and she had eight brothers and sisters. Her greatest friend was her sister, Cassandra, who was two years older. Later, the family moved to the fashionable town of Bath. People came to Bath to drink the waters for their illnesses and to find husbands for their daughters. Jane didn't enjoy Bath very much; she was pleased to move back to Hampshire in 1809.

Jane's family was a loving one and made the most of the parties, dinners and dances that took place in the country. Jane received several offers of marriage but did not accept any of them. She lived quietly and spent much of her time writing. *Sense and Sensibility* (1811) was her first successful book. Next came *Pride and Prejudice* (1813). Jane wrote both these books some fifteen years before they appeared for sale. Two more books followed: *Mansfield Park* (1814) and *Emma* (1816). After her death, two other works, *Northanger Abbey* and *Persuasion* came out.

Jane Austen died in Winchester at the early age of forty-two.

Jane Austen's books describe, with a quiet but sharp sense of fun, a world she knew well: middle-class families with daughters in need of husbands. The perfect husband is young and handsome, loves music and literature, and is good at dancing. More importantly, he has plenty of money and a fine country house. Each book describes the dance of love between young ladies and gentlemen. The wars in Europe at that time do not enter the picture. All attention is on the game of love – a much more serious business.

A film of *Sense and Sensibility* was made in 1996, with Emma Thompson, Kate Winslet and Hugh Grant in the main parts. Other stories by Jane Austen in Penguin Readers are *Pride and Prejudice*, *Emma* and *Persuasion*.

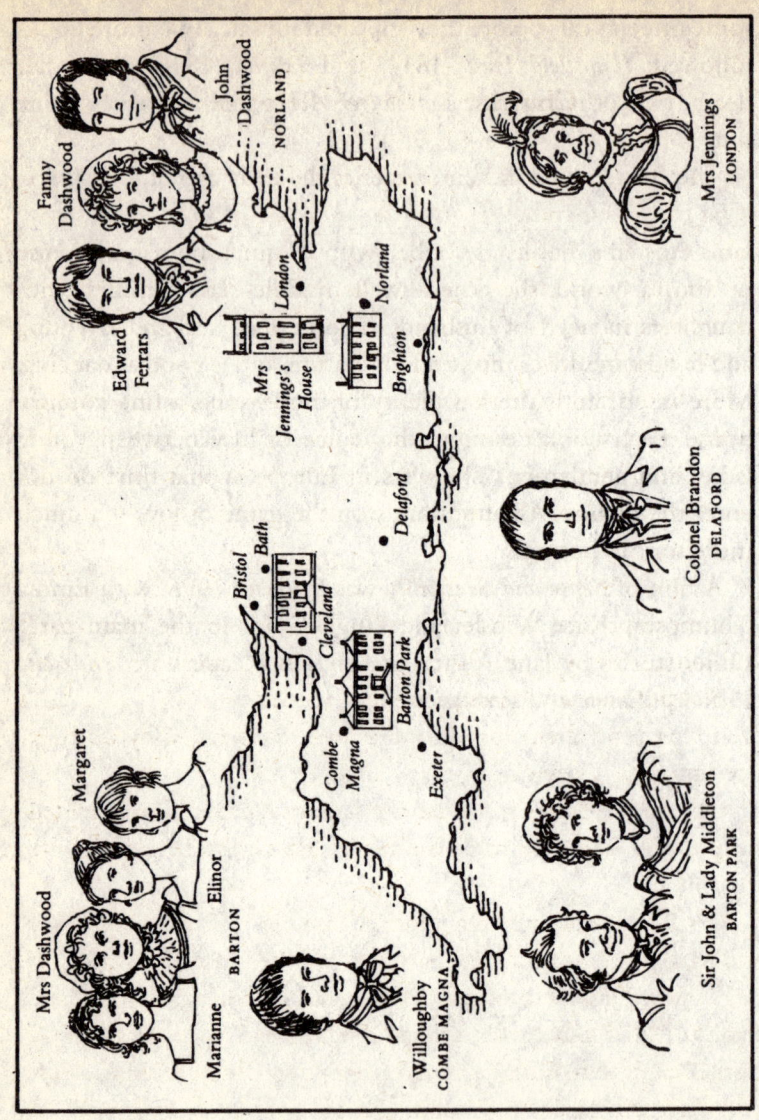

## Chapter 1  A New Home

'I'd like to help my sisters,' said John Dashwood. 'My father asked me to do something for them, so I shall give them some money.'

'Oh, but your father was ill!' Fanny, his wife, answered. 'He didn't mean it!'

'But I promised! They need my help.'

His father was dead now and everything was changing in the family. John was the son of Mr Dashwood's first wife; he had plenty of money from his mother, and Fanny was also quite rich. But Mr Dashwood did not have much to give his next wife and their three daughters.

'Well – perhaps we can give them a present,' said Fanny.

'A small present of money – that's a good idea. You're right!' said John.

'No, not money. First, help them to find a new home. And then later send them some fruit, or fish, or meat. Why do they need money? They can live very cheaply!'

'Of course! Yes, that's what my father wanted,' John decided happily. He was not a bad man, but he listened to his selfish wife too much.

Mrs Dashwood and her three daughters – Elinor, Marianne and Margaret – would soon have to leave their family home. This large house, called Norland Park, now belonged to John and Fanny. Mrs Dashwood disliked Fanny, and wanted to leave immediately, but Elinor advised her not to. Elinor was nineteen, and very sensible. She thought carefully about everything. Her mother wanted to move to another large house, but they had to find somewhere cheap.

And so they stayed at Norland for a few more months, living

like visitors in their old home. Fanny's brother, Edward, was also staying there. He was not handsome, but he was a pleasant, clever young man. He and Elinor were often together, and were soon good friends. Mrs Dashwood noticed this.

'In a few months,' Mrs Dashwood said to Marianne, 'Elinor and Edward will get married! Elinor will be so happy!'

'But what shall we do without her?' Marianne asked.

'We'll see her often! But you look sad, Marianne. Don't you like Edward?'

A quiet, serious person like Edward was boring to Marianne. 'Oh, he's a kind man. But he doesn't seem to feel strongly about books and music, or Elinor's beautiful pictures! I must have a different kind of man! But will I ever find one?'

'My dear girl, you're only sixteen!' Mrs Dashwood replied.

In fact, Elinor did like Edward very much. But his sister, Fanny, did not like seeing them together. She and her mother, Mrs Ferrars, wanted a rich wife for Edward, not a poor one like Elinor.

Fanny was rude to Mrs Dashwood about this, 'He is not free for *any* young lady, you know. My mother has special plans for him.'

Mrs Dashwood could not wait to leave Norland.

She was lucky. A letter arrived from Sir John Middleton, a relative from Devon, in the west of England. He wanted to offer her a house not far from his large house, Barton Park. It was a friendly letter and they agreed to move there. The new house was cheap and they could live there easily. Mrs Dashwood still hoped for some money from John, but he did not give them anything. They sold their horses and carriage, and only took three servants with them. 'Dear, dear Norland!' cried Marianne. 'Perhaps I shall never see you again! And oh, you beautiful trees! When shall I walk under your leaves again?'

'He is not free for any *young lady*, you know.'

# Chapter 2  An Invitation to Dinner

It was a long way to Devon. But it was a very pretty part of the country, with high hills, fine trees, and open farmland. Their new home had two sitting-rooms and four bedrooms, and was quite comfortable. They put Marianne's piano in one of the sitting-rooms, and some of Elinor's pictures on the walls.

'It's too small,' Mrs Dashwood said, 'but I'll save some money and build more rooms.'

The next day, after breakfast, Sir John Middleton came over to see them. He was about forty, and seemed to be a naturally happy, friendly man. He invited them to dinner at Barton Park, and later sent them some fruit and vegetables from the garden.

Barton Park was a large, handsome house with plenty of servants, about half a mile from their new home. Sir John nearly always had visitors there, and often gave dances too. He liked people, and Lady Middleton liked to serve beautiful meals. But she was a cold woman, who did not say much.

At dinner, they met Mrs Jennings, the mother of Lady Middleton. She was very different from her daughter — a large, happy woman, who talked a lot, and liked to laugh loudly.

'Did you two girls leave your hearts at Norland?' she asked Elinor and Marianne. Both Mrs Jennings's daughters were married, and so she now wanted to marry off the rest of the world! 'Oh, your faces are red,' she laughed.

The other visitor at Barton Park that evening, was a quiet man of about thirty-five. His name was Colonel Brandon and he was a friend of Sir John's. He had a sensible face; he was not handsome, but he was a gentleman.

After dinner, Marianne played the piano and sang, and he was the only person who really listened. Everybody enjoyed the music, but Sir John talked all the time, and Lady Middleton was only interested in her four noisy children. They came in after dinner, pulled her dress and stopped the conversation.

'Colonel Brandon is old,' thought Marianne, 'but he likes my music.'

'He loves her!' thought Mrs Jennings. And soon she told everybody this.

'What a stupid idea!' Marianne said to her mother later. 'How can he feel anything? He's thirty-five years old – an old man!'

'I'm only forty!' Mrs Dashwood laughed. 'And I'm not ready to die yet!'

'Well, perhaps he's not ready to die. But at his age, he can't know anything about love! He needs a nurse, not a wife!'

## Chapter 3   The Handsome Stranger

The Dashwoods were now busy and happy in their new home. The girls often went out walking, and one day Marianne and Margaret decided to climb a high hill together, near the house. It was a beautiful morning when they left, but soon black clouds built up in the sky, and it started to rain very hard. They began to run fast down the hill. Margaret got to the bottom, but Marianne fell and could not get up again.

A gentleman was walking near them with his dog. He saw the accident, and immediately came to help them.

'I've hurt my foot!' Marianne said.

'I can carry you,' he replied, and picked her up from the ground. He carried her down the hill, through the garden and into the house. Elinor and her mother were very surprised to see this young man with Marianne in his arms, but he quickly explained everything.

'I can carry you,' he replied, and picked her up
from the ground.

'Oh thank you, thank you!' Mrs Dashwood said again and again. 'Please sit down!'

'No, I'm too dirty and wet from the rain,' he answered. 'But can I come tomorrow? My name is Willoughby.'

He was a handsome young man, and Mrs Dashwood encouraged him to visit them again. And Marianne quickly forgot about her bad foot.

'Do you know this man Willoughby?' they asked Sir John the next day.

'Willoughby? Is he here again? Yes, he's a good man! He rides a horse well and has a clever little dog! Was the dog with him?'

But they were not interested in his dog.

'Who is he?' asked Elinor. 'Does he live here?'

'No, no – he has a relative here, an old lady. He has a very nice house not too far away, at Combe Magna in Somerset, and will be a good husband for somebody! Be careful Elinor – Marianne has Brandon already. She mustn't catch all the men! Perhaps Willoughby will be just right for you!'

'My daughters do not try to catch men!' Mrs Dashwood said angrily.

'Last Christmas,' Sir John continued, 'I invited him to one of my dances, and he danced from eight in the evening until four in the morning!'

'Did he?' asked Marianne. 'That's the kind of man that I like!'

And Willoughby liked the three Miss Dashwoods. He visited them the next day. The two older sisters were both pretty girls; Marianne was taller than Elinor, and had a specially lovely face with a sweet smile and dark, bright eyes. She was shy at first. Then Willoughby saw the piano and talked about music, and Marianne could not stay silent. After this, he came to the house every day.

Sir John also invited the girls to several dances at Barton Park, and Willoughby and Marianne danced together most of the time. It was a happy time for Marianne, and she did not try to keep her feelings a secret.

'My girls will soon have two good husbands,' Mr Dashwood thought. Marianne forgot about Colonel Brandon, but he did not forget her. Elinor liked him, and was sorry for him, but what could she do? Can a quiet gentleman of thirty-five win against a handsome young one of twenty-five?

One day, there was a plan to visit Whitwell, a fine house with some beautiful gardens. Some friends of Colonel Brandon lived there. Everybody planned to drive there in carriages from Barton Park — the Middletons, the Dashwoods, Colonel Brandon, Willoughby, and a few more friends too. They all arrived at Barton early, and were looking forward to the day's adventure.

But during breakfast, Colonel Brandon came in with a letter. He looked unhappy.

'I'm very sorry,' he said, 'but I must go to London immediately to finish some important business. We can't go to Whitwell today. My friends are away, and the servants don't know you — you won't get in without me.'

This was an unpleasant surprise.

'Well,' Lady Middleton said, 'you'll be back soon, and we'll go to Whitwell then, won't we?'

'Perhaps I won't be able to return. I can't be sure.'

'We can still go out in the carriages,' Sir John said. 'It's a beautiful day.'

Willoughby said quietly to Marianne, 'Some people don't like this kind of happy party, and Brandon is one of them.'

He and Marianne jumped into their carriage and drove away very fast. The others also drove off and did not see Marianne and Willoughby again until much later.

There was a dinner, and a small dance at Barton Park for everyone that evening. Mrs Jennings sat next to Marianne, and Elinor could hear their conversation.

'And so you had a secret adventure this morning! But I know all about it!'

Marianne turned red in the face.

'We went out in my carriage,' Willoughby said quickly.

'Ah, but where to? To Allenham!' Willoughby's old aunt lived in Allenham House, but she was away from home that day. 'To the house that will soon be yours!' She laughed. 'Do you like it, Marianne? It's very big, isn't it?'

Marianne could not speak.

'Is this true?' Elinor asked her later.

'Yes, of course it's true! And why not?'

'You and Willoughby went together to this empty house! Oh, Marianne, that wasn't right!'

'It was the nicest morning that I have ever spent! What's wrong with that?'

'If something is nice, it can still be wrong,' Elinor replied quietly.

Mrs Dashwood soon heard the news. 'They're engaged!' she decided. 'He took her to see her new home!'

But Willoughby and Marianne did not tell them anything.

'Ask them, please, mother,' Elinor said anxiously to Mrs Dashwood. 'Are they really engaged? And why is it a secret?'

'Ask her!' repeated Mrs Dashwood. 'No, I can't! I'm sure Marianne will tell me soon. Perhaps Willoughby's aunt doesn't like Marianne. Perhaps they must keep the engagement secret for a few months.'

'I'm not sure. Maybe there *is* no engagement.'

'But he loves her! You can see that.'

'Yes, I can. But I don't understand – there's something strange about it all.'

A few days later, Mrs Dashwood, Elinor and Margaret were coming home from a visit to Lady Middleton.

'Look!' Margaret said. 'There's Willoughby's carriage outside our door!'

The ladies went inside, and immediately Marianne came out of the sitting-room and ran upstairs to her bedroom. She was crying. Willoughby was still standing in the sitting-room. He looked very serious.

'Is Marianne ill?' Mrs Dashwood asked anxiously.

'No – I hope not. I'm sorry – I'm here to say goodbye.'

'Goodbye? Are you going back to London?'

'Yes, this morning.'

'Well, you'll come back soon!'

'Unhappily, that won't be possible. I only see my aunt once a year.'

'But we can invite you! You're always welcome here!'

'You're very kind,' Willoughby said. 'But – I must go now.'

He climbed into his carriage, and drove away.

## Chapter 4  A Secret Engagement

Marianne was very unhappy, but she also enjoyed her sadness a little. She did not sleep, eat or speak much. She cried a lot. She liked to walk round the park and think of Willoughby. She sang the songs that they sang together when he was there. She read again the books that they both enjoyed.

One day, the three sisters were out walking along the road to Barton. A man on a horse was riding towards them.

'It's Willoughby!' Marianne shouted. She started to run towards him.

'No!' called Elinor. 'It's somebody different – oh!'

It was Edward Ferrars. He was on his way to visit them, but he seemed uncomfortable with them.

*It was Edward Ferrars. He was on his way to visit them,
but he seemed uncomfortable with them.*

'Have you just arrived?' Marianne asked him.

'No. I came two weeks ago,' he answered.

Two weeks ago! Why didn't he come to see Elinor then?

'Did you visit Norland?' Elinor asked.

And why were Edward and Elinor so cold together? Marianne asked herself. They were not like *real* lovers! Not like her and Willoughby!

'Yes, about a month ago.'

'How did it look?' Marianne asked him.

'Oh, as it always looks in autumn – plenty of dead leaves everywhere.'

'Those beautiful leaves!' Marianne said. 'Oh, I would love to see them again! Nobody there enjoys them!'

'Not everyone likes dead leaves,' said Elinor.

'Well then, Edward, do you like the beautiful hills here?' asked Marianne.

'Yes, but the roads at the bottom will get very dirty in winter.'

'How strange!' Marianne thought, and so did Elinor. What was wrong? She was unhappy about Edward's coldness, but she did not want to show her feelings.

Edward stayed at their house for a week, and was more friendly by the end of it. But there was still something different about him.

'Perhaps there's trouble with his mother,' Elinor thought.

'She wants me to be famous!' Edward told them once. 'But I only want some quiet, useful work. I'd like to be a priest and work for the Church.'

Elinor was not happy after his visit, but she worked busily in the house, and seemed calm.

One morning, Sir John arrived at their door, and invited them up to the house.

'Please come now!' he asked them. 'Come and meet two

beautiful young lady visitors! You'll like them so much! They're two sisters, relatives of Mrs Jennings . . .'

Miss Lucy Steele, the younger sister was really quite pretty. The older Miss Steele,★ was about thirty, and her face was neither sensible nor pretty. They were playing with Lady Middleton's children.

'John loves being a bad boy!' said Lady Middleton happily. Her oldest child took Miss Steele's handkerchief and threw it out of the window. 'And William is so playful!' William was now biting the lady's finger. 'Little Anna Maria,' continued Lady Middleton lovingly. 'She's always so quiet!' Just then, the little girl hit her head on the table and began to scream. The Miss Steeles gave her sweets and Lady Middleton took the crying child out of the room.

'What fine, clever children!' said Lucy Steele. 'I don't like very quiet children.'

'Quiet children can sometimes be very pleasant,' Elinor replied.

'Do you like Devon, Miss Dashwood?' said Miss Steele. 'Did you want to leave Norland? There were some handsome and amusing young men there, weren't there?'

'I'm sorry, but I really don't know,' said Elinor. She did not like the two sisters – Lucy Steele was not so free with her words as the older Miss Steele, but her face was not very honest. But the Miss Steeles liked the Miss Dashwoods, and Elinor and Marianne now had to spend an hour or two with them nearly every day.

During one dinner at Barton Park, Miss Steele said to Elinor 'It's very good news about your sister! Engaged so young and to a very handsome man! Perhaps you will be lucky too soon! Or perhaps you already have a special friend?'

★Jane Austen calls the older sister 'Miss Steele' and the younger 'Miss Lucy Steele'.

*The secret escaped quickly from Sir John's lips.
'The letter F –,' he said.*

The secret escaped quickly from Sir John's lips. 'The letter F –,' he said. 'That's a very important letter for Elinor!' Everybody laughed.

'But who is it?' Miss Steele asked.

'His name is Ferrars! And it's a great secret!' He spoke into her ear, but everybody could hear.

'Oh, what a nice young man!' said Miss Steele to Elinor. 'I know him very well.'

'Not *very* well,' Lucy said quickly. 'We saw him once or twice at my uncle's.'

'You know him?' Elinor asked. 'How interesting!'

But she could not find out anything more that evening. Then, a few days later, she and Lucy were walking in the park together.

'Do you know Mrs Ferrars?' Lucy asked suddenly. 'What kind of a woman is she?'

'Fanny's mother? No, I've never met her.'

'I want your advice – you see, maybe she will soon be a relative of mine.'

'Of yours?' Elinor said in surprise. 'Do you know her younger son then – Mr Robert Ferrars?'

'No,' Lucy said, 'no – I speak of Edward Ferrars, the older brother.'

Elinor could not speak, but her face changed colour.

'You're probably surprised,' Lucy continued, 'because it's a great secret. You see, we're engaged. Our engagement started four years ago.'

'And when did you meet?'

'Oh, we were only children then. Edward often stayed in my uncle's house.'

'I'm so surprised!' Elinor said. 'Are we talking about the *same* Mr Edward Ferrars?'

'Here – look! ' Lucy took a small picture from her pocket. It was Edward's face.

'You will keep my secret, won't you?' said Lucy. 'Only you can advise me! I love him so much, but his mother is a difficult woman — I'm not rich enough for her. Edward and I are so unhappy. We can't meet often, and we can only write letters about twice a year. What can we do?'

'I'm sorry,' Elinor said, 'but how can I help you?'

'His mother won't give him any money. He was very unhappy on his last visit to Barton, wasn't he? Didn't you notice?'

'Yes, we did.'

'Elinor, you seem cold! Have I said something wrong?'

'It's very difficult for you both, and I'm sorry for you.' Elinor tried to speak calmly.

'Must we break our engagement? Tell me, Elinor! Must we wait for years like this?'

'You have waited four years already.'

'If Edward gets some money, we *will* be happy, I know it! Can you ask your brother? Would he give Edward the job of priest in the church at Norland?'

Elinor felt sorry for Edward. Did he really love this young woman? 'Mr Ferrars is my friend,' she said, 'and I want to help him. But my brother won't listen to me.'

'Will you be in London this winter, Miss Dashwood?' Lucy asked.

'No, we can't possibly go,' Elinor replied.

'Oh, but I'd like to see you there. My sister and I are going to stay with some relatives. But of course, I'm really going there to see Edward — he's coming in February.'

## Chapter 5    An Unkind Letter

Elinor was wrong about London. Mrs Jennings lived in London for part of each year, and she invited the two older Dashwood girls to visit her there in January. Mrs Dashwood agreed immediately.

'You two must go! Margaret and I will be very happy here together with our books and our music. Mrs Jennings is a kind and motherly sort of woman.'

'Mother, there is a problem –'

'Ah, my sensible Elinor sees a problem, of course!'

'She's a good woman, but not the politest –'

'Elinor, if you don't go, I will!' said Marianne. Marianne, of course, was hoping to see Willoughby in London. 'And you'll enjoy it too! Edward will be there.'

'Yes, you can meet his mother! She'll be your mother too, one day,' Mrs Dashwood said happily.

They arrived in London after a three-day journey in Mrs Jennings's carriage. Her house was large and comfortable. The girls had a very pleasant bedroom, and Elinor immediately began to write a letter. Marianne was writing too.

'I'm writing to Mother,' Elinor said, 'and so you need not write to her today.'

'I'm not writing to her!' said Marianne quickly.

'She's writing to Willoughby', thought Elinor.

Marianne finished the letter, and gave it to a servant to take. All evening, she listened for a knock at the door. At last there was a visitor – but it was only Colonel Brandon. Marianne ran out of the room.

'Is your sister ill?' he asked Elinor anxiously.

'Oh – no – she's just tired, and she has a headache,' Elinor told him. Poor man! she thought.

He talked politely for some time, and then asked her, 'Will you be pleased to have a new brother soon?'

'What do you mean?' asked Elinor.

He tried to smile. 'Well, everybody knows about Marianne's engagement.'

'I just want to know – have Willoughby and Marianne agreed everything? Will they marry soon?'

'Everybody? That's not possible! Her family don't know about it – how can other people think this?'

'I'm sorry. I didn't mean to be rude. I just want to know – have Willoughby and Marianne agreed everything? Will they marry soon?'

Elinor could see his love for Marianne clearly, and so she tried to explain everything to him. It was better to be honest; there was not much hope for Colonel Brandon.

No other visitor came, and there were no letters for Marianne during the next few days. Marianne wrote another letter to Willoughby, but there was no reply.

'This is very strange,' Elinor thought. She decided to write home. Her mother *must* ask Marianne about the engagement.

A few days later, they all went to a party. It was a large party, with crowds of well-dressed people, and the room was very hot. Elinor found two chairs for them by the wall. Suddenly she saw Willoughby. He was standing near them, talking to a young lady.

Marianne saw him too. Light came into her face, and she jumped up. Elinor pulled her down again.

'Sit down! Be calm!' she ordered.

'Why doesn't he come and speak to me?' Marianne asked.

'Perhaps he hasn't seen you yet.'

Then Willoughby turned round and looked at them. He held out his hand – but to Elinor, not Marianne.

'Willoughby! What does this mean?' Marianne asked. 'Didn't you get my letters?'

He looked very uncomfortable. 'Yes, thank you. You kindly sent me news of your arrival.' Then he turned away to the young lady again.

Marianne's face was white now. 'Go to him, Elinor! He must explain! Surely there's some mistake!'

'No, my dear sister. It's not possible now. Wait until tomorrow.'

But the next morning early, Marianne was up and writing a letter. She was crying hard.

'Marianne, can I ask –?'

'No, Elinor, don't ask me anything. Soon you will know everything.'

Before lunch, a letter came – a reply from Willoughby. Marianne took it to her room, and Elinor followed. Her sister was lying on the bed, almost screaming in pain. Elinor took the letter and read it: 'I am sorry, but you must understand. I am engaged, and will soon get married. I do not want to hurt your feelings, but you have perhaps made a mistake. I did not mean to encourage you. My feelings for you were never those of a lover.'

'Oh, this is unkind!' Elinor said. 'This is not the letter of a gentleman!'

Mrs Jennings was waiting downstairs; she was planning to take them out.

'Ah, Marianne got a letter from Willoughby this morning!' she laughed. 'Poor Marianne looks quite ill with love! He must marry her soon!'

'Mrs Jennings,' Elinor said, 'they are not engaged!'

'Oh yes, my dear Elinor – it's not really a secret, is it? I tell everybody about it!'

Elinor told her the bad news. It was a very unpleasant surprise for Mrs Jennings, and she tried to do many kind things for Marianne all day. She brought her a glass of wine, gave her the best place by the fire, and cooked little bits of the nicest food for her. Marianne could not enjoy any of this.

'How can he do this, Elinor?' she said to her sister that evening in their bedroom.

'He's a bad man. If he breaks your engagement, it will be better finally. You'll see.'

'There was no engagement!'

*Her sister was lying on the bed, almost screaming in pain.*

'No engagement?' Elinor asked, surprised. 'But he loved you, didn't he?'

'Yes – no – he never said it. But he *seemed* to love me, and he encouraged me to love him, too. What has happened? Who is this woman? Oh, Elinor, you are so lucky! You can be happy – I can never be happy again!'

'Me, happy? Marianne, you don't know – and of course I can't be happy! Not when you are in so much pain.'

The next morning, Mrs Jennings brought them news about Willoughby's young lady. 'She is a Miss Grey, and very rich. And so he's broken his promise just for money!'

'Well, there was no real engagement between Willoughby and Marianne –'

'No, don't try to explain it. He's not a gentleman. But there's one good thing – Colonel Brandon can have her now. He'll be a very good husband! And he has a fine house at Delaford in Dorset with fruit trees in the garden – I'll encourage him at once! She'll soon forget about Willoughby.'

Colonel Brandon came to the house often, and was a good friend both to Elinor and Marianne. Marianne did not show any interest in him, but she was not unkind to him. She felt only her terrible pain. Soon Willoughby got married, and the news only made it worse. She wanted to leave London, but her mother didn't advise it. There was more to do in the city, Mrs Dashwood wrote in her letter, and their brother, John Dashwood, was coming to town soon. They must see him.

The Middletons were also in town. 'I shall never speak to Willoughby again!' Sir John said. Lady Middleton was polite, but a little cold, which was not unusual. In fact Elinor found this easier. Too many people were anxious about Marianne, and talked about her all the time.

And then the Miss Steeles arrived in London.

'You *are* in London, then!' Lucy said to Elinor. 'I thought so!'

Elinor understood her meaning very well, but said nothing.

## Chapter 6   A Family Disagreement

Soon after this, their brother, Mr John Dashwood came to see them at Mrs Jennings's house. Colonel Brandon was there too that morning.

'And so you're all happy in your new little home at Barton! Edward told us all about it. I must meet the Middletons. Will you take me to meet them, Elinor?'

Elinor agreed. It was a fine day, and they could walk the short way to the Middletons' house.

'Colonel Brandon seems to be a good sort of man – a gentleman! Does he have money?'

'Yes, and a large house.'

'Wonderful! He'll be a good husband for you, Elinor!'

'For *me*?' Elinor asked in surprise.

'Oh yes! I watched him – he looked at you a lot!'

'No,' Elinor said, 'he doesn't want to marry me!'

'You're wrong, Elinor, wrong! You must try! You haven't got much money, it's true – but he'll have you, I'm sure! We'll all be very happy for you. Perhaps my sister and Fanny's brother will both marry at the same time!'

'What do you mean?' Elinor asked quickly. 'Is Edward going to marry someone?'

'We think so, yes, very soon. His mother has found the right young lady for him. Her name is Miss Morton, and she is very rich. And money is so useful – everything is very expensive now. We need more money for Norland.'

'Yes, John – but you're not poor.'

'Well, we're not rich! We're making a new flower garden, and of course we had to buy more furniture. Your mother took so

'What do you mean?' Elinor asked quickly. 'Is Edward going to marry someone?'

much with her! Now, what is the matter with Marianne? She doesn't look well. She must be careful, if she wants to find a husband!'

Lady Middleton and Mrs John Dashwood were soon the best of friends. They were both selfish women. The Dashwoods invited the Middletons to dinner with Elinor, Marianne, Mrs Jennings, the Miss Steeles and Colonel Brandon. They invited Mrs Ferrars too.

'Oh, Elinor! I'm so anxious! Only you can understand this! I shall soon meet my new mother!' Lucy Steele said, entering the Dashwoods' house.

'Not yours, but Miss Morton's perhaps,' Elinor thought. Edward was not there – she was pleased. He was in London already, but could not come that evening.

Mrs Ferrars was a little, thin woman with a serious and quite unpleasant face. She did not say much, but looked at Elinor with dislike.

There were many servants, and the dinner was an expensive one. Later, in the sitting-room, John Dashwood showed one of Elinor's pictures to Colonel Brandon.

'How well Elinor paints!' he said. The Colonel agreed.

'Yes,' said Fanny, 'look, mother! Have you seen Miss Dashwood's picture?'

'Very pretty,' Mrs Ferrars said coldly, and did not look at it.

'It is a little like one of Miss Morton's pictures, isn't it?' Fanny continued.

'*She* paints beautifully,' Mrs Ferrars said, more warmly now. 'Miss Morton does everything well!'

Marianne didn't like this. 'Well, and who is this Miss Morton? And what does she matter? *Elinor* is here – we are talking about her, not Miss Morton!'

Mrs Ferrars and Fanny were both very angry. But Colonel Brandon looked lovingly at Marianne. She put her arm round her sister and said quietly, 'Dear, dear Elinor! Don't be unhappy!' And then she began to cry.

'Ah, poor girl!' Mrs Jennings said.

'Poor Marianne,' her brother said to Colonel Brandon. 'She was quite beautiful a few months ago, but now it's all gone.'

Lucy Steele was very excited. She came to see Elinor the next morning.

'I'm so happy!' she said. 'Mrs Ferrars was so kind to me! Did you notice? Everything will be all right. I know it will!'

Marianne still didn't know anything about Edward's and Lucy's engagement. 'I must tell her soon,' Elinor thought.

The time for this came very quickly. One morning, Mrs Jennings hurried back into the house after her shopping.

'Have you heard the news?' she asked Elinor. 'Oh, it's so strange! Edward Ferrars and Lucy Steele are secretly engaged! And now Mrs Ferrars has heard about it! She is very, very angry. She has a rich young lady ready for Edward. Your sister Fanny shouted at Lucy, Lucy cried, and Mrs Ferrars has sent Edward out of the house! She is not going to give him any money – she's going to give it all to Robert!'

Robert, Edward's younger brother, was a well-dressed, but quite stupid young man.

'Lucy isn't rich! But she's my relative, and a nice young lady!' Mrs Jennings continued. 'Why can't they marry? Well, Edward is keeping his promise! He won't break the engagement – he has told his mother this. Poor young man! If he has no home, he can stay here!'

Elinor went to tell Marianne. 'How long ago did you hear about their engagement?' Marianne asked. She and Elinor were both crying now.

'Four months ago.'

'Four months! And you said nothing to me! All the time I was so unhappy and you were so kind to me! Oh, Elinor!'

'All the time I was so unhappy and you were so kind to me!
Oh, Elinor!'

'I wanted to say something, but it was a secret. And perhaps they will be happy together – I hope so.'

'How can you forget him so easily? Is your heart so hard?'

'Marianne, I do feel strongly for Edward. Yes, I loved him, and it was very painful. Fanny, Lucy and Mrs Ferrars have all hurt me too. But I couldn't say anything – I had to try to be calm, and to help you too. Please, Marianne, say nothing, and be polite to Lucy and Edward.'

Marianne kissed her sister warmly, and promised.

## Chapter 7   All's Well That Ends Well

Marianne wanted to go home very much now, after two months in London. It was a long journey, quite difficult and expensive. But, luckily, Mrs Jennings offered them her help. Her other daughter, Charlotte, lived at Cleveland, only one day's journey from Barton, their home. Mrs Jennings wanted to visit her for Easter.

'We can travel there together,' she told the girls, 'and stay a few days. Then your mother can send her servant for you. Colonel Brandon is coming too. We shall have a happy time!'

'Oh no,' Marianne said to Elinor. 'I can't go there – Cleveland is in Somerset! Willoughby's home is near there.'

Elinor talked about their mother – 'We shall see her very soon!' and at last Marianne agreed.

But first Colonel Brandon came to see Elinor about Edward.

'I don't know Mr Ferrars well,' he said, 'but I met him a few times and liked him. He's going to be a priest, isn't he? Well, I can offer him work in my church at Delaford. The money is not much, and the house is quite small, but it's better than nothing. Will you tell him?'

Elinor was very surprised, but she agreed. That same morning, she took pen and paper, and began to write him a letter. Then suddenly the door opened, and Edward came in.

They both found it difficult to speak. 'You're leaving London,' he said. 'I wanted to say goodbye to you.'

Elinor explained the Colonel's offer to him.

'The Colonel has asked me to be his priest? Is it possible?'

'You still have friends – are you surprised?'

'No – you were always a good friend –'

'It is really Colonel Brandon's idea, not mine,' Elinor replied. 'But I'm very pleased about it.'

'I'll go and see him immediately!' Edward said, jumping up.

'And now he can marry Lucy,' thought Elinor sadly.

Elinor visited her brother for the last time in London.

'Has Colonel Brandon *really* given the job of priest to Edward?' he asked her. 'Why did he do that?'

'He wanted to help Mr Ferrars.'

'Well, Edward is a very lucky man! And now he will marry Lucy. But Mrs Ferrars mustn't hear about it!'

'Of course she'll hear about it!' Elinor said.

'Ah, but she'll be so unhappy! Edward is still her son!'

'But she's forgotten that, hasn't she?'

'No, no – she is the most loving mother in the world!'

Elinor was silent.

'Possibly,' her brother continued, 'Mr *Robert* Ferrars will marry Miss Morton now.'

'Can't she choose?' asked Elinor. 'Or are Robert and Edward the same to her?'

'Of course it's the same thing! Robert will have all the money now.'

♦

Early on an April morning, they began their journey to Cleveland, and arrived there after three days. The house was large and modern, with beautiful trees round it.

*Marianne enjoyed walking among the trees, thinking sadly of Willoughby, and his house only thirty miles away.*

Marianne enjoyed walking among these trees, thinking sadly of Willoughby, and his house only thirty miles away. She walked through the wet grass and far away into the wilder part of the park. After four days, she caught a terrible cold.

At first, Elinor was not worried.

'Marianne must go to bed and sleep all night. Then she'll be better in the morning,' she told Colonel Brandon. He was much too anxious about her.

For a few days, it was just an ordinary cold. But then Marianne got much worse. She had a terrible headache and a fever, and began to say strange things.

'Is mother coming?' she asked anxiously. She lay heavily in her bed; it was about midnight. 'Oh, but if she goes round by London, I shan't see her! It's too far!'

Elinor sent for the doctor immediately. Her sister looked very ill. And who could go for their mother?

'I'll go,' said Colonel Brandon, and left at once.

Elinor sat with Marianne all night; the doctor didn't come until five o'clock in the morning.

'It's a dangerous fever,' he said. But he couldn't really help her. Everyone was very frightened now.

'She's a beautiful young girl!' Mrs Jennings cried. 'She can't die so young!'

Elinor tried to stay calm, but it was too much for her. The doctor came again.

'No, she's not better,' he said. Marianne was unnaturally quiet now, and sleeping heavily. 'Perhaps I can still help her – I'll give her some different pills.'

By about midday, Marianne was a little stronger, and the fever not so bad. By four o'clock, she was much better.

'She's out of danger now,' said the doctor, and Marianne began to sleep more comfortably.

Elinor ate some tea with Mrs Jennings, their first meal of the day. Then Mrs Jennings went up to bed. They were both very tired, but Elinor wanted to wait for her mother. She heard a carriage outside. But it was only eight o'clock – her mother and Colonel Brandon could not possibly arrive until ten. Who was it?

The door opened, and Willoughby walked in.

'I must talk to you, Miss Dashwood!'

'And I must *not* talk with you, Mr Willoughby!'

'Please! – it's very important, I've come all the way from London today!'

'Today?' said Elinor, surprised. 'Well then, sit down, and tell me your business at once. But please be quick!'

'How is your sister? Is the fever really better now? Your servant told me – is it true?'

'Yes, we hope it is.'

'And now, Miss Dashwood, am I a bad man or a stupid man? Bad – that's what you think, isn't it? But no, I'm not really bad, only stupid. And I'm very sorry – I want to tell you everything.'

He told her his story. He didn't mean to love Marianne. She was a pretty girl, and he amused himself with her at first. Then he started to love her seriously. He planned to marry her. But his old aunt, who lived near Barton, heard something terrible about him: he once took a young woman away from her husband, and then left her when she was having his baby.

'If this is true, Allenham House will never be yours!' she told Willoughby.

It was true; he had very little money, and was waiting for his aunt's house to be his.

'I have always spent a lot of money,' he told Elinor now. 'It's not good, I know. My happiest hours were with your sister, and I loved her, but I couldn't live without money. And so I decided to forget her, and to marry Miss Grey. My heart was hard then.

Then of course I saw you in London, and that was terrible! Marianne's sweet face – did you see the letter?'

'The letter that you wrote to her? Yes.'

'My wife wrote it. She found Marianne's letters, and was very angry. I held the pen, but they were all her words.'

'This is wrong!' Elinor said. 'Don't talk about your wife like that! You chose her – you chose all this!'

'My wife didn't love me then, and she doesn't love me now. I heard about Marianne's illness, and at once my love for her came back into my heart! I love only her! But she will never be mine now. Will you tell her all this? I hurt her badly, but I have also hurt myself. Am I still a very bad man? What do you think?'

'I'll tell her something. And I'm sorry for you, Mr Willoughby.' Perhaps he was not a very bad man, but he was a weak and selfish one, and he liked money too much.

Elinor sat thinking hard while she waited for her mother. At last Mrs Dashwood arrived with Colonel Brandon. She was very frightened, but Elinor quickly told her the good news that Marianne was better, and she ran upstairs to see her. She held her daughter in her arms, and offered to sit with her all night. Elinor was glad to agree; she needed to sleep now.

Her mother had something more to say the next morning. 'Elinor! Colonel Brandon opened his heart to me yesterday and told me about his love for Marianne. We were both in the carriage, and so frightened about her fever – it was natural to speak about our feelings for her! Oh, he is a good, unselfish man!'

'Yes,' Elinor replied, 'he is. If Marianne agrees to marry him, I'm sure they'll be very happy. What did you say to him?'

'I encouraged him – "You need time, just time, Colonel!" I told him. Marianne won't think about Willoughby for ever. Well, he's not so sure, but he's ready to wait. She'll be very near me at Delaford! The Colonel is not as handsome as Willoughby, but he's a much better man.'

'I love only her! But she will never be mine now.'

Every day now Marianne got a little better, and at last they were able to return to their house at Barton. Marianne was happy to be home again, but remembering everything was painful too. She went to her piano, and picked up some music. But it was a book of music with Willoughby's name in it, and she couldn't play.

'Well, Elinor,' she said. 'I'll be stronger soon, and then I shall study seriously. I shall read for six hours every day, and practise the piano. I'll learn a lot this way.'

Elinor smiled. One morning, she took Marianne out for a walk. Marianne looked up at the hill behind the house and said, 'I first saw Willoughby there. I can talk about it now – most of the pain has gone. But I *would* like to know – did he really love me? Or was it all a terrible mistake?'

Elinor told her about Willoughby's visit. Marianne turned white, but said, 'Thank you! oh thank you! It will be easier now!'

Soon Margaret returned from a visit, and Mrs Dashwood and her daughters were together again in their home.

Then, one day, one of the servants returned from the nearest town and said, 'Mr Ferrars is married. Did you know?'

Marianne began to cry, and Elinor looked terrible. Mrs Dashwood saw the pain on her face, and began to question the servant.

'Who told you this?'

'I saw Mr Ferrars and his new wife, Miss Lucy Steele. Their carriage stopped outside the hotel. Miss Steele – well, Mrs Ferrars now – told me. "I've changed my name!" she said. Mr Ferrars didn't say much.'

'Where were they going?'

'They came from London, and they were travelling west.'

'They're probably going to visit Lucy's uncle,' said Elinor quietly.

'She looked very well,' the servant continued, 'and very happy too. She's a handsome young woman!'

Elinor had no hope now. Before this day, there was always just a little hope. But now Edward was married – and so quickly, too! He wasn't a priest yet.

And then, through the window, they saw a man on a horse. Was it the Colonel? He was coming to visit them very soon. But, no! – it was Edward. Everyone saw, and waited silently. 'I *will* be calm,' Elinor told herself.

Edward looked white and anxious too, but Mrs Dashwood gave him her hand. 'We hope you will be very happy,' she said.

Elinor began to talk about the weather. Then she had nothing more to say, so Mrs Dashwood spoke again.

'Is Mrs Ferrars well? Is she with her uncle now?'

'She's well, thank you – but with her uncle?' He looked surprised. 'No, my mother is in London.'

'My mother is talking about Mrs *Edward* Ferrars,' said Elinor.

'Perhaps –' Edward said, 'perhaps you mean Mrs *Robert* Ferrars?'

'Mrs *Robert* Ferrars!' Marianne and her mother said together. But Elinor could not speak.

'Yes – my brother and Miss Lucy Steele are married now. Perhaps you haven't heard.'

Elinor jumped to her feet and ran out of the room.

Three hours later, she and Edward were engaged, and he was the happiest man in the world. He told her all about his engagement to Lucy.

'I was staying with her uncle some years ago,' he said, 'and I had nothing to do. I wanted to study, but I couldn't go to university for another year. And so I thought only about Lucy and her pretty face. We were much too young for an engagement. But I had to keep my promise.'

'But how did Lucy and Robert get married?' Elinor asked.

'Perhaps —' Edward said, 'perhaps you mean Mrs Robert Ferrars?'

'Robert went to talk to Lucy. "You can't marry Edward!" he told her. "It's very bad for the family!" He went to see her two or three times more – and you can guess the rest! He was pleased to take her from me. And I didn't have enough money for her. My mother is very angry with them, but Robert is still her favourite, and she'll give him something.'

Edward agreed to stay at their house for a week, and he and Elinor had some very happy days together. They talked about everything.

'But Edward,' she said, 'you were engaged to Lucy, and you spent a lot of time with me! Wasn't that wrong?'

'At first you were just a friend, but then I began to realize my feelings for you. Yes, it was dangerous – I had to leave, but I couldn't leave you at once,' he said.

Colonel Brandon arrived, and the two men were soon good friends. Edward would be the priest for the Colonel's village soon, but money was still a problem for him and Elinor. They did not need a lot, but they did need enough to live on.

Then John Dashwood wrote to her: 'Mrs Ferrars wants to see Edward again! She is ready to forgive him.'

'Yes, but she doesn't know about our engagement,' Edward said. Finally, he went to visit his mother. She was very glad to see him. Elinor was not as good as Miss Morton, but at last she agreed to his new engagement. She gave them enough money so that they could marry comfortably.

After the wedding, John Dashwood visited the happy pair in their new home. 'Well, dear sister,' he said. 'You *are* lucky, it's true. But I would prefer to have Colonel Brandon for my brother! He has a much better house! Perhaps Marianne – he doesn't love her yet, but maybe he will soon – you must encourage her, Elinor! Yes, you must encourage them both!'

Marianne was a very unusual girl. She loved a man when she was old enough to love him deeply. But she finally forgot him, and married another! She was nineteen then. And her new husband, Colonel Brandon, you will remember, was already 'an old man'! But they were very happy together, and Marianne soon loved him with all her heart.

Mrs Dashwood continued to live at Barton, but went to see her two daughters very often. They were, of course, living near their mother – Marianne in Delaford Park, and Elinor in the priest's house in the village. And Mrs Dashwood wasn't unhappy at home. Margaret was old enough to go to dances now, and her mother could think about a husband for her, too.

# ACTIVITIES

## Chapters 1–3

*Before you read*

1 Look at the pictures in this book. Which of these activities can you see in them? Write 'yes' or 'no' for each.
   - **a** riding
   - **b** swimming
   - **c** reading
   - **d** playing the piano
   - **e** sleeping
   - **f** carrying somebody
   - **g** walking along the street
   - **h** crying
   - **i** greeting
   - **j** sitting in a carriage

2 These words all come in this part of the story. Use a dictionary to check their meaning.

   *advise   anxious   carriage   encourage*
   *engaged   gentleman   sensibility   servants*

   Now choose the right meaning for each one from the list below:
   - **a** a vehicle used before the age of cars
   - **b** a polite, well educated man
   - **c** worried and unsure
   - **d** to tell somebody what you think they must do
   - **e** to tell somebody that they are doing the right thing
   - **f** promised in marriage
   - **g** person employed to cook or clean in someone's home
   - **h** full of sad or happy feelings

*After you read*

3 Who are these people?
   - **a** a sensible girl aged nineteen
   - **b** her brother's wife; she is rather rude
   - **c** a large, happy woman who talks a lot
   - **d** a sixteen-year-old girl who likes music
   - **e** a quiet, sensible man of about thirty-five
   - **f** a handsome young man who likes dancing

4 Answer these questions:
   a How does Marianne hurt her foot?
   b Who carries her home?
   c What interests does he share with Marianne?

**Chapters 4–6**

*Before you read*
5 What do you think the title of the book means? How does the writer show 'sense' and 'sensibility' in the story? Discuss your ideas with other students.
6 Choose the right answer.
   One of the young men wants to be a priest. A *priest* is:
   a a doctor of animals
   b a churchman
   c an adviser on the law

*After you read*
7 Answer these questions:
   a Why is Marianne so deeply unhappy about the news in Willoughby's letter?
   b What do we know about his 'young lady'?
   c Which visitor often comes to Mrs Jennings's house to see the sisters?
8 'You *are* in London, then,' Lucy says to Elinor. 'I thought so'. What deeper meaning does Elinor understand in these words?
9 Why is Mrs Ferrars angry with Edward and how does she punish him?

**Chapter 7**

*Before you read*
10 Choose the right answer.
   A *fever* means an illness with:
   a a high temperature
   b bad pains in the stomach
   c difficulty in sleeping

11 Work with a partner.
   *Student A*: You are Elinor. Ask Marianne why she is 'almost screaming with pain' over Willoughby's letter. Then try to give her sensible advice.
   *Student B*: You are Marianne. Tell Elinor about Willoughby's letter.

*After you read*

12 Who says these words? Who to?
   **a** 'I wanted to say goodbye to you.'
   **b** 'I love her. But she will never be mine now.'
   **c** 'You need time, just time.'
   **d** 'Did he really love me? Or was it all a terrible mistake?'
13 Answer these questions:
   **a** 'Elinor had no hope now.' Why not?
   **b** How do her feelings suddenly change?
   **c** Where do Elinor and Marianne live at the end of the story?

**Writing**

14 Which do you prefer to have as a friend: Colonel Brandon or Mr Willoughby? Say why.
15 You are Marianne. You met Willoughby for the first time yesterday. In your personal record book, describe what happened. Write about your feelings too.
16 Which people in this story are specially interested in money? Give examples of their interest. Are they good people or bad people?
17 Some people think that the writer's 'message' in this book is that strong feelings can be dangerous. Do you agree? Say why or why not.

---

Answers for the Activities in this book are published in our free resource packs for teachers, the Penguin Readers Factsheets, or available on a separate sheet. Please write to your local Pearson Education office or to: Marketing Department, Penguin Longman Publishing, 5 Bentinck Street, London W1M 5RN.